SLOT MACHINES

AND

COIN-OP GAMES

SLOT MACHINES
AND
COIN-OP GAMES

*A Collector's Guide to One-armed Bandits
and Amusement Machines*

BILL KURTZ

CHARTWELL
BOOKS, INC.

A QUINTET BOOK

Published by Chartwell Books
A Division of Book Sales, Inc.
110 Enterprise Avenue
Secaucus, New Jersey 07094

This edition produced for sale in the U.S.A.,
its territories and dependencies only.

ISBN 1-55521-731-1

This book was designed and produced by
Quintet Publishing Limited
6 Blundell Street
London N7 9BH

Creative Director: Terry Jeavons
Designer: Nick Cannan
Project Editors: Damian Thompson,
David Barraclough
Editor: Peter Arnold
Photographer: Ian Howes
Contributor: Dick Bueschel

Typeset in Great Britain by
Central Southern Typesetters, Eastbourne
Manufactured in Singapore by Eray Scan Pte. Ltd
Printed in Singapore by Star Standard Industries Pte. Ltd.

*This book is dedicated to the
memory of my father, Julius
Kurtz, who took me to my first
arcade – and always had a
pocketful of dimes for me to
spend there.*

Contents

Introduction

There's something magical about playing coin-operated amusement machines.

You can become a big-league baseball star or save the Earth from outer space invaders. You can pilot a helicopter, outdraw a western desperado or drive a grand prix racing car. All this for a pocketful of loose change. Coin-op machines offer more adventures than you could ever hope to experience in real life. You can live out your fantasies in the comfort of your neighbourhood game room, free from the routine and responsibility of work and family.

Slot Machines and Coin-op Games looks at some of the best-loved amusement games ever produced, along with some that you've never heard of. If you've ever spent any amount of time with these mechanical wonders, you'll probably find some of your favourite games here. We'll cover all of the most popular types of coin-operated amusements, and take a look at what the future may hold. You'll even find some helpful tips about buying games for your home!

Coin-op games have always been popular, but only in the last two or three decades have they become socially acceptable. The Great Depression of the 1930s spawned the first penny arcades, which catered for people who needed an inexpensive way to escape their problems. Most offered small prizes such as cigarettes and candy to high-scoring players. For only a penny, players could escape from the harsh realities of the world around them. Coin-op games were also found in taverns, barbers' shops and cigar stores – in fact, anywhere men congregated. Before long, arcade machines picked up a seedy, unsavoury image which stuck for years.

Coin-op games became a symbol of the 1950s, a time when post-war mechanization was sweeping the country. People were fascinated by machines, and teenagers especially loved coin-op games. Although the machines were often found in 'wholesome' settings like coffee bars and restaurants, they were still considered less than respectable. Even today, we often picture a leather-jacketed teenager with slicked-back hair playing pinball when we think of the 1950s.

In the sixties, arcades started appearing in enclosed shopping precincts. For the first time, young children could play arcade games that previously had been found only in adult-oriented locations. Youngsters could finally spend hours with these mechanical wonders for a pittance – and mall arcades were a hit with parents who left their children surrounded by games while they did their shopping.

Arcades flourished throughout the seventies and eighties as futuristic electronic games with digital scoring, space-age sounds and high-tech video screens hooked a new generation of players. Some arcades even began to resemble miniature amusement parks, and people lined up for games that lifted you into the air and spun you around.

In some places, though, arcade machines have been banned for more than half a century. Because some of the coin-op games of the thirties paid out coins or dispensed prize tickets to skilful players, they were classified as 'gambling devices' and outlawed in many communities.

In *Slot Machines and Coin-op Games*, we'll look at the complete array of machines designed purely for

LEFT *Back in the 1950s, games like Chicago Coin's* Hooligan Pool *were played by leather-jacketed hoodlums in dingy taverns and smoke-filled pool halls; today's games are often enjoyed by rising professionals in brightly decorated arcades.*

ABOVE *Prize-filled cranes and iron-claw digger machines were popular in the twenties and thirties, but were outlawed in some areas, where they were considered to violate the gambling laws.*

amusement – even the one-armed bandits and other machines which award cash or prizes are included, as they are part of the total coin-op experience. The line between gambling and amusement was always thin. A good example are the old iron-claw diggers that were so popular in the 1930s and forties. You could walk away from one of these iron-claw machines with a small prize – a pack of playing cards or a comb, for example – so they, too, were branded as gambling devices. Still, most players consider these claw machines to be games of skill; why else would so many people spend $8.00 (£4) in change to win a prize that costs $1.29 (65p)?

Other coin-op machines were really gambling devices disguised as amusement games. They could award literally hundreds of replays (up to 999, in some cases) which were usually paid off in cash 'under the table' by the location owner. Bally and United produced a number of bingo machines that closely resembled pinball games, except that they had no flippers. You shot five balls which rolled into 25 numbered holes; the corresponding numbers would light on one or more bingo cards pictured on the backglass, with the same winning combinations found in real bingo. The more coins you deposited at the game's start, the better your odds of winning – and your pay-off in replays would also increase.

Many of the oldest arcades in the US can be found in the resort towns on the shorelines of the east and west coasts of the country. Some have been welcoming players since the late 1920s, and even include machines that are over 50 years old! While nearly every arcade today is geared towards the younger video game players, you can still find a few vintage machines in operation in arcades in such summer resort areas as Seaside Heights, New Jersey, and Geneva-on-the-Lake, Ohio. Antique gypsy fortune teller machines await the chance to predict your future, and old-time Kiss-O-Meters will let you know if you're 'hot stuff' or 'ice cold'. Many of these antique games still operate on nickels and dimes – and some even take pennies – so you can play these old-time machines at old-time prices.

#111 Castle Cafe
Joe Mogel, Prop.
Ciudad Juarez, Mexico.

It's impossible accurately to estimate how many different coin-operated amusement games have been produced. Because of their ever-changing popularity, anywhere from 100 to 400 new machines are introduced annually. In the last five decades, that adds up to at least 10,000 different games!

Until a few years ago, playing coin-op games was regarded by some non-players as a waste of time; these people couldn't appreciate the pleasure of manipulating a mechanical device. Recently, though, these machines have been recognized as true pieces of Americana, and the designers who create these devices that give so much happiness to so many people are finally getting the credit they deserve. Game pioneers like Harry Williams, David Gottlieb, Ray Maloney, Sam Stern and Steve Kordek are taking

ABOVE During Prohibition Americans who lived close to the border could always get a drink across the line. These Yankees are at the Castle Café in Juarez, Mexico. Slots along wall are Mills' Operator Bell (1925) and Skelly's The Fox (1926).

their rightful places in arcade game history, while some of today's designers, including Mark Ritchie, Barry Oursler and Dennis Nordman are becoming as well known as the machines they've created.

Most coin-op games are popular for only a short period of time (if at all), so game manufacturers have to introduce new models every few weeks to retain players' interest. So while you may find ten of Williams Electronics' new *Fun House* pinball machines in your neighbourhood this month, you may have difficulty locating even one of them a few years from now!

People play arcade games for a variety of reasons. Some find them relaxing, while others enjoy the physical rush they get from playing the machines. But most players agree that coin-op machines offer a welcome break from everyday life. You're able to suspend reality for a short time and enter a make-believe world where anything is possible. You can go from flying a spaceship to entering a medieval jousting match as quickly as you can step from one machine to another. And if at first you don't succeed . . . there's always the next game.

Both arcade games and slot machines require no previously learned information or physical skills. You don't have to memorize mathematical formulae or go on a low-fat diet to play. You just need concentration and some free time – and, of course, a few spare coins!

ABOVE *Used games from the 1940s often sold for less than $100 in the mid fifties; today, some collectors will pay thousands of dollars for these same machines.*

LEFT *Thousands of new and used machines are sold each year to amusement game operators around the world. Game distributors like this one may have hundreds of machines in their inventory.*

CHAPTER 1
Penny Arcade Machines

Coin-operated games have been around for more than a century. They've endured through two world wars, a depression and the computer age. They've amused four or five generations of players and continue to entertain millions of people each year.

The first popular coin-operated machines, produced in the 1890s, were pay-out gambling games. These one-armed bandits, coin-op roulette wheels and other games of chance offered players the opportunity to double or triple their money if luck was with them – but it was usually the gambling machines' owners that came out ahead.

At the turn of the century, the first true coin-op amusement games appeared. For only a penny, players could turn a crank and watch a series of photos or slides flip by like a movie. The entire show took less than a minute, with subjects ranging from westerns to comedies to cops and robbers. People loved being able to view 'moving pictures' any time they wanted to, and these mutoscopes, as they were called, were an instant hit; they were found in candy stores, tobacconists', drugstores and other places where people shopped. Several companies produced updated and replacement flip shows for mutoscopes, and for more than two decades, viewers were fascinated with these devices; their popularity dropped when 'talking' movies appeared in the late 1920s, although they could still be found in many penny arcades throughout the thirties and forties. A few nostalgic reproduction mutoscopes are produced periodically by today's game manufacturers, using old-time subjects and stars like Charlie Chaplin.

In the 1920s, other amusement devices began appearing. Since coin-op machines were played mostly by men, strength and grip testers were among the

LEFT In the 1920s, mutoscopes like this one were the hottest coin-op machines around, but their popularity dropped in the thirties and forties when pinball machines and other novelty games came into circulation.

BELOW D. Gottlieb & Co., the leading pinball manufacturer for many years, was founded in 1927 when David Gottlieb began producing strength and grip testers in a small factory in Chicago. In the 1920s, nearly every tavern, cigar store and barber shop had one of these small machines.

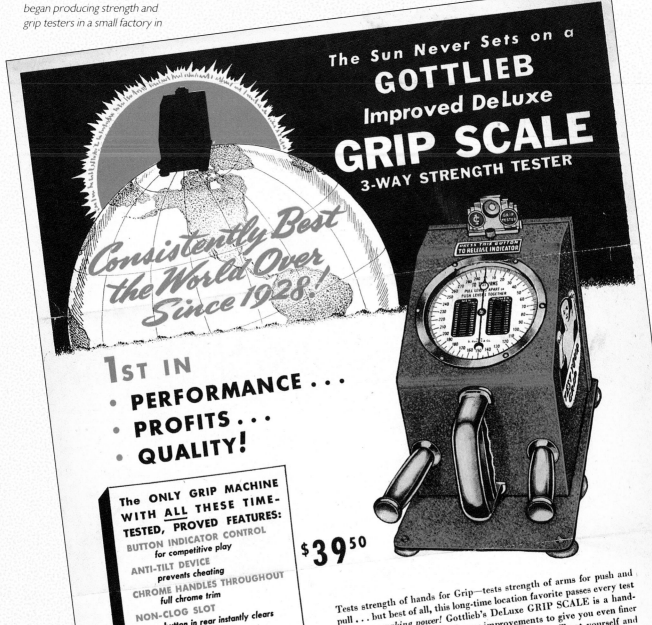

most popular devices. Squeezing or pulling a metal handle activated a dial or meter that would tell you how strong you were. One of the most unusual strength testers was produced by the International Mutoscope Company in the 1920s. This large upright machine was over six feet tall – and had a full-size donkey's head at the top. You stood on the base and pulled upward on the handle to measure your strength; the more you lifted, the louder the donkey brayed! Another unusual strength tester, also produced by the International Mutoscope Company, featured an animated donkey at the bottom of a tree; the harder you pulled, the higher the monkey would climb. You could find out if you were a 'Superman' or just a 'Coconut Crusher'.

Exhibit's *Fist Striker* was a different kind of strength-testing device. You simply hit a striking pad (a sponge rubber disc covered with soft leather) with your fist. The machine recorded the force of your blow; a strong hit would ring a bell and light up the word 'champion'. According to Exhibit, *Fist Striker* 'will get the money out of a Wooden Indian'.

Like most coin-op games of the 1920s, many early strength testers were completely mechanical and used no electricity – all of the action was regulated by gears and springs. But when game manufacturers began producing electrically operated machines near the end of the decade, a new era began.

Many of the new machines were not actually 'games', because players simply deposited their money and watched as the devices sprang to life. For only a penny, you could see a crying baby or watch an execution carried out by tiny mechanical soldiers. One of the most inventive machines was a coin-operated, self-playing banjo! For a penny, you could watch a glass-encased banjo play one of six different songs, each lasting about a minute. Metal 'fingers' would pluck the strings, playing tunes like 'Camptown Racers' and 'Swanee River'.

RIGHT *Mechanical fingers plucked the strings of the Self-playing Banjo, produced in the* *1920s and popular in small taverns which couldn't afford a proper jukebox.*

In fact, players also paid for the privilege of getting shocked! Several electric shock machines were produced that encouraged players with phrases like 'Electricity Is Life'. One machine, for example, had two metal knobs that you held as long as you could while a mild electrical charge was flowing. If you could hang on long enough – usually about a minute – a bell would ring to let everyone around you know what you had accomplished. Some companies even produced 'Electric Chairs' which would deliver a mild shock that the manufacturer called 'invigorating'. Although it may seem strange to us today, these electric shock machines were among the most popular coin-op amusements of the 1920s and 1930s.

Until the late twenties, coin-op machines were simply an interesting diversion; if you had an extra penny or two in your pocket after you bought your groceries, you might drop it into the mutoscope on your way out of the store. But by the end of the decade, people had started going out of their way to play these machines when penny arcades began operating. Even during the Depression, these arcades remained popular. Interestingly, many of the coin-op machines built after the mid 1930s took nickels rather than pennies, but the name penny arcade stuck anyway.

Fortune-telling machines started appearing in the early 1930s, and are still popular today. They're among the most beautiful and captivating of all coin-op devices, with ornately carved wooden cabinets and large glass windows. Many fortune-telling machines featured a full-sized manikin inside a glass booth that appeared to come to life when a penny was inserted. These lifelike manikins, often shown only from the chest up, appeared to breathe, blink and nod their heads as they contemplated your future. After a few seconds, a card containing your 'fortune' would appear. Because most of the manikins were old women surrounded by tarot cards, tea leaves and crystal balls, the machines were nicknamed 'gypsy fortune tellers', although bearded men, cats and even pigs told fortunes, too. Newer gypsy fortune tellers featured knobs that let you select your sign of the

ABOVE People loved to be shocked – literally – when they played machines like this Electric Energizer, produced in the 1920s. The mild electrical current was considered 'invigorating' and even healthy in those days.

GRANDMOTHER'S PROPHESIES

13

Beware of Friday the 13th
That's your unlucky day
Whenever it rolls around
Bolt the doors and indoors stay.

You are meticulous in your habits and that has brought happiness to you and those about you. You have a fine mind and though you haven't had much formal education and have developed your brain to a great extent. You are extremely devoted to your family and would let no stone go unturned if you could help your friends. People appreciate your good nature, and your true friends are legion. Your generosity has become a by-word amongst your friends. Don't overdo it.

Drop another Coin in slot and I will tell you more.

Your Lucky Numbers - 152 - 53, 54, 55, 56
Copyright 1944, Mike Munves Corp., New York

LEFT *Their high standard of craftsmanship and styling have made gypsy fortune tellers like this one among the most sought-after arcade machines around. Some collectors will pay thousands of dollars for these machines today.*

zodiac, so that you could receive a more personalized fortune. Watching one of these old-time games in operation is like seeing a waxworks figure come alive; it's eerily compelling to watch, even though you know it's just an elaborate machine.

ABOVE The Mystic Pen was one of the more unusual fortune-telling machines of the 1920s; your 'personal' fortune was 'handwritten' for you by a large fountain pen that bobbed up and down for a few seconds behind a glass window.

RIGHT By turning a selector knob on the outside of the coffin-shaped cabinet, you could ask 'Ramasees the Great' questions like 'Will I Be Rich?' when you dropped a penny into this unusual machine, built by Exhibit Supply in the thirties.

Other fortune-telling machines were not quite as elaborate. Some would simply illuminate a slide with a fortune or proverb when you looked into a peephole, while others had flashing lights that would blink for a few seconds before giving you a fortune card. Fortune-telling scales first appeared in the early 1930s, and remained popular for several decades. For only a penny (later a nickel and then a dime), you could learn, not only about your future, but also your weight. In the seaside resorts of Britain, these machines were gradually ousted by 'real' crystal-ball-glazing 'gypsies' and Tarot card readers.

'Love testers' were also popular in the 1930s. Several companies produced these devices, which let you press a button or grip a handle, and then told you about your love life or sex appeal. No skill was

necessary to operate a love tester, gypsy fortune teller or many other penny arcade machines; the flashing lights and animated figures provided the entertainment.

Exhibit Supply Company, established in 1901, was one of the leading manufacturers of penny arcade machines in the twenties and thirties. Many of their products were actually cleverly disguised vending machines that sold picture postcards of movie stars, while others dispensed humorous documents such as marriage certificates and 'any old license to do any old thing'. Some cards answered questions like 'How Many Babies in your Wedding Ring?' and even told you 'How to Become Popular, Attract the Opposite Sex and Become a Great Lover'. Exhibit began producing these card vendors in the 1920s and called them 'the backbone of the penny arcade business' because they were so popular. Even after Exhibit stopped making coin-operated games in the late fifties, the company continued to produce postcards and documents for its old machines because so many were still in operation.

There were also some competitive penny arcade games built in the 1920s and 1930s. One of the earliest was *Football*, produced by the Chester Pollard Company. Two players stood side by side in front of the cabinet, which housed 20 tiny animated figures in a glass-enclosed arena. Operating the control handles on the front of the cabinet moved the figures, which kicked a small ball towards the soccer-style goal areas at both ends of the cabinet. The metal figures were durable but finely crafted, with hand-painted faces and cloth jerseys.

RIGHT A perennial arcade favourite, today's Skee Ball machines are almost identical to those produced in the thirties and forties, like this model built by the Philadelphia Toboggan Company. Most Skee Ball machines reward skilful players with tickets which can be redeemed for prizes.

Most of the coin-operated machines of the 1920s were made of cast iron, but by the thirties, all were made of wood and many had large glass windows to showcase the action. Most of the animated figures were hand-crafted and painted, giving the machines a personal touch that you don't find on today's games.

Many penny arcade games of the 1930s and early 1940s rewarded players for their skill; some paid out in coins while others awarded tickets which could be exchanged for cash or prizes. Among the most popular ticket-dispensing games were skee ball machines. Every penny arcade of the thirties had a row of skee balls, and a display case, crowded with prizes like glassware and small toys, where you traded in your tickets for prizes. Skee ball machines have remained virtually unchanged over the last 60 years (except for mechanical improvements). Skee ball has been a perennial favourite and it's still popular today.

Still, many US local law enforcement officials considered skee balls and other coin-op games to be gambling devices because they could award something of value, and the games were banned from many arcades by the late thirties. Some cities allowed a limited number of machines into a location, but only if the operator could prove conclusively that the games couldn't possibly be used for gambling. Several novelty arcade games were developed specifically for areas where coin-op machines weren't welcome. For example, Bally's promotional material for its 1940 *Baskets* arcade game read, 'No prizes are ever awarded on *Bally Baskets* ... it is absolutely impossible to set up any kind of award schedule on the game. Designed for amusement and competitive skill play only, *Bally Baskets* is legal in the strictest sense of the word ... opens the tightest closed territory ... insures you substantial steady profits and permanent operating security. Local authorities are favourably impressed by the fact that no prize award system can possibly apply to *Bally Baskets* ... no unethical operator can possibly create unfavourable publicity by offering prizes.' Actually, *Bally Baskets* was a rather popular game – and it was completely mechanical and needed no electricity. Two players

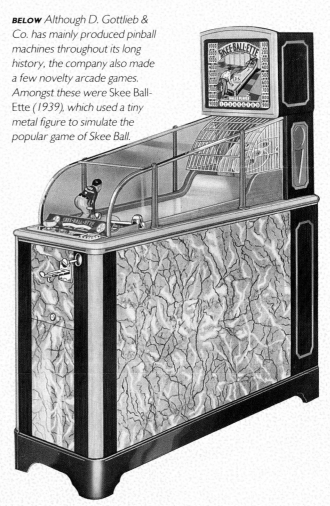

BELOW *Although D. Gottlieb & Co. has mainly produced pinball machines throughout its long history, the company also made a few novelty arcade games. Amongst these were Skee Ball-Ette (1939), which used a tiny metal figure to simulate the popular game of Skee Ball.*

manipulated a small bouncing ball inside a glass-enclosed arena and tried to bounce it into one of the baskets mounted inside the cabinet. Several similar games were produced by other manufacturers during the 1960s and 1970s.

Another popular 1940 machine was Exhibit's *Candid Camera*, a large metal box-type camera mounted on a stand. *Candid Camera* contained a wavy, fun house-type mirror which would light up for a few seconds when you put in a coin.

Players loved mechanical animation in the thirties, and Evans' *Ski-Ball* was one of the most popular of these games. *Ski-Ball* was based on the popular arcade game, and featured a small, metal player-controlled manikin that rolled a tiny ball towards a series of scoring cups inside a glass-enclosed cabinet. Pinball giant D. Gottlieb & Co. produced a similar machine called *Skee Ball-ette* in 1940.

RIGHT *Countertop games were popular in the 1920s. These small machines used no electricity, and were usually found in candy shops, drug stores and other places where there was no room for full-sized coin-op games.*

Non-electric countertop games were produced throughout the thirties and forties. Many were shooting games with pistol-grip mechanisms that fired tiny metal pellets. The action on these small devices couldn't compare to full-sized arcade machines, but they were popular in restaurants, bars and other places where standard coin-op games couldn't fit.

Coin-operated machines were just as popular in Europe as they were in the United States. Companies like Bryan's Works of England produced several penny arcade machines, including some that performed magic tricks; one machine, for instance, would 'cut' a piece of string, only to have it reappear in one piece. Another British company produced several animated machines (including *The Haunted Churchyard* and *The Miser's Dream*) which contained small figures that moved around the glass-enclosed booth to enact a short story with a 'surprise' ending. Mutoscopes were also popular in England in the 1920s and 1930s, although the shows were racier and more revealing than their US counterparts; they were often titled 'What the Butler Saw' and featured scantily clad women in lacy underwear. Many British arcades also contained 'fruit machines', one-armed bandits and other gambling devices that were outlawed in the United States.

Some of today's best-known producers of coin-operated equipment have been around since the thirties. Bally Manufacturing, now a part of Williams Electronics, introduced its first pinball machine in 1931 before branching out to other coin-op games. D. Gottlieb & Company was formed by David Gottlieb in 1928, and now operates under the name Premier Technology; although the company is best known for its pinball games, it started out by manufacturing grip testers. And jukebox companies like Rock-Ola and Seeburg have each produced several penny arcade amusement games in the last 60 years; in fact, Rock-Ola was one of the leading manufacturers of early pinball machines, coin-op scales and counter-top games before the company decided to specialize in jukeboxes in the late thirties.

The coin-op games industry was thriving when World War II ended production. After the war, only the most popular types of amusement games – baseball machines, gun games, pinballs and bowling machines – went back into production. 'Passive' machines like love testers and mutoscopes (which had long since passed their prime) were replaced by skill-oriented novelty arcade games that encouraged competition. Arcade games had emerged from their infancy and entered into their adolescence.

ABOVE What Is My Weakness was one of the many fortune-telling machines produced by the Exhibit Supply Company in the thirties and forties. Exhibit made reference to these machines as 'the backbone of the Penny Arcade business'.

21

COUNTERTOP GAMES

Not all coin-op games are large, heavy machines with a lot of complicated mechanical or electronic parts inside. Some games are designed to fit on a countertop, and take up less space than a microwave oven or portable TV.

After more than 60 years, you can still find countertop games in a few bars today. These small machines were popular in candy shops and grocery stores in the 1920s and 1930s, but before long, no bar was complete without at least one of them.

Most of the countertop games built before World War II were completely mechanical, and often contained marbles or tiny metal balls that you shot into scoring holes with a spring-controlled lever or knob. These games usually played very quickly – sometimes less than 30 seconds – and demanded very little skill.

Many types of full-sized arcade machines were available as counter games. Keeney's *Texas Leaguer*, a countertop baseball game built in the mid fifties, was one of the most popular. Many countertop games were miniature shooting galleries, and contained small guns that fired metal pellets at an assortment of targets. In the late forties and fifties, electrically operated counter games became common, and by the seventies, several popular video games – including *Space Invaders* and *Head-On* – were available in countertop cabinets.

Early countertop machines used four suction cups to keep the games in place, although today's machines are usually anchored to the counter on a swivel base so that two people can compete. The control panels and screens on countertop video games are a bit smaller than full-sized arcade machines, though, and some players have difficulty adjusting to the change.

Although countertop games aren't nearly as popular today as they were 30 or 40 years ago (largely because of the versatility of sit-down cocktail table video games), a few companies still produce these machines. Players are attracted by the novelty of a small coin-op game that they can play from the comfort of their bar stool. Because these machines are less expensive than full-sized arcade games, we'll probably continue to find countertop machines in places that don't have enough space for larger games.

ABOVE Up to four people could play Four Square at once because there were four identical playboards on each side. Some arcades mounted the machine on a pedestal.

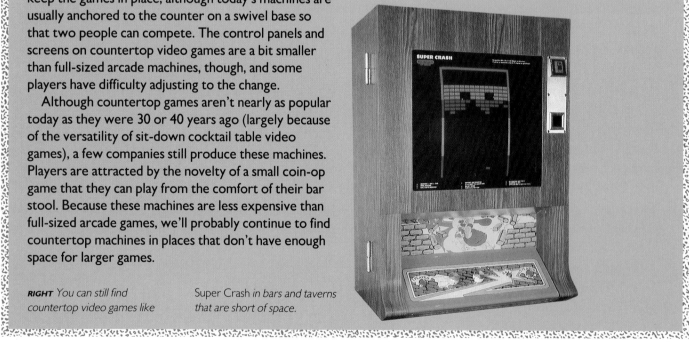

RIGHT You can still find countertop video games like Super Crash *in bars and taverns that are short of space.*

22

CHAPTER 2
Baseball Machines

Baseball has always been one of the United States' favourite pastimes, and coin-operated baseball machines have always been among the most popular arcade games. Baseball machines blend skill, timing and a little bit of luck in an easy-to-understand game that appeals to players of all ages.

At first glance, you might mistake a baseball machine for a pinball game because they're so similar in size and shape. On closer inspection, though, you'll find that they're completely different. Instead of the bumpers and spinners found on pinball games, most baseball machines have only a row of targets or pockets across the top of a wide-open playing field, with a single bat at the bottom of the field rather than a pair of flippers. After the ball is released from a trapdoor in the centre of the playboard, the bat is swung, sending the ball into the targets, marked 'single', 'double', 'triple', 'home run' – and, of course, 'out'. Naturally, the home run targets are the hardest

to hit, while the 'out' targets are the easiest. And, as in real baseball, you can swing the bat only once after each ball was released; an early or late swing would register as a strike. Usually, the game lasts three innings, with three outs allowed per inning.

The first baseball machines appeared in the early 1930s. One of the most popular was Rock-Ola's *All Star Baseball* (1932). This game actually included tiny metal figures on the field, and featured a colourful stadium backdrop around the playfield. The 'outfielders' even shifted from side to side in front of the scoring pockets, adding realism to the game – and making it a bit harder to score.

Western's *Baseball* (1935) was billed as having 'All the thrills, suspense and action of an actual baseball game.' Instead of animated figures, this game had a series of flashing lights on the playfield, indicating the runners' positions. By eliminating the costly animated figures, Western was able to undersell its

LEFT *Notice the careful attention that was paid to detail on the miniature players in Rock-Ola's 1932* All Star Baseball. *The pitcher even hurled the steel ball through the air towards the bat.*

ABOVE Williams' Deluxe Short Stop (1958) had a unique bonus feature. Each time a player scored a grand slam, a letter of Short Stop would light; completing the name of the game would be rewarded by several replays.

baseball machines every year (usually in the spring, just in time for the start of the season), Williams has been the leading baseball manufacturer since the 1950s. Williams' innovations – including backbox animation and variable pitching speeds – have kept their machines the most popular, even today.

Still, other manufacturers have produced some rather interesting baseball machines, too. Genco's *Champion Baseball* (1956) and *Hi-fly* (1957) were both very unusual games, because they used large plastic balls which were shot through the air toward the bat, rather than the usual small steel balls that rolled along the playfield. *Champion Baseball* and *Hi-fly* also featured upper-deck scoring, with several vertical rows of targets at the top of the playfield; an 'over the fence' hit scored 50 runs!

United's *Super Slugger* (1955) not only featured triple-deck scoring and backbox animation, but also included batting control. For the first time, players could swing the bat weak, medium or hard, depending on the control button they selected. Before long, United (and the other manufacturers) also included pitching controls, letting players select curve balls, fast balls or sliders.

During the fifties, baseball machines were designed for up to six players. Chicago Coin's six-player *Super Home Run* (1954) was one of the first multiple-player games, although by the end of the decade, most baseballs were designed for one or two players. Many of these two-player models allowed one player to pitch to the other while varying the speed of the ball to fool his opponent. Unlike most two-player coin-op games, both players could participate simultaneously rather than taking turns at the controls.

The late 1950s and early 1960s are considered by some coin-op collectors to be the golden age of baseball machines. Williams' *Pinch Hitter* (1959), for example, not only had backbox animation and a choice of pitches, but a game-to-game carry-over feature as well; each grand slam would light a letter of *Pinch Hitter* on the backglass, and completing the name scored a replay.

One of the most attractive post-war baseball

competitors, making *Baseball* one of the best-selling baseball machines of the thirties.

Very few baseball machines were produced during the wartime years, but by the end of the decade, new models began appearing. Williams' *Super World Series* (1950) was a landmark game, with its introduction of backbox animation. *Super World Series* featured a small baseball diamond in the backbox, visible through the backglass. For every hit, a tiny metal player appeared in the diamond and circled the bases. While these animated players were simply flat cut-outs rather than the elaborate three-dimensional figures found in *All Star Baseball*, their movements corresponded to the playfield scoring, giving *Super World Series* a new element of realism. Even the backglass artwork was unique, with the animated baseball diamond seen through the perspective of a television broadcasting booth (complete with a CBS-TV cameraman!).

Although several game companies released new

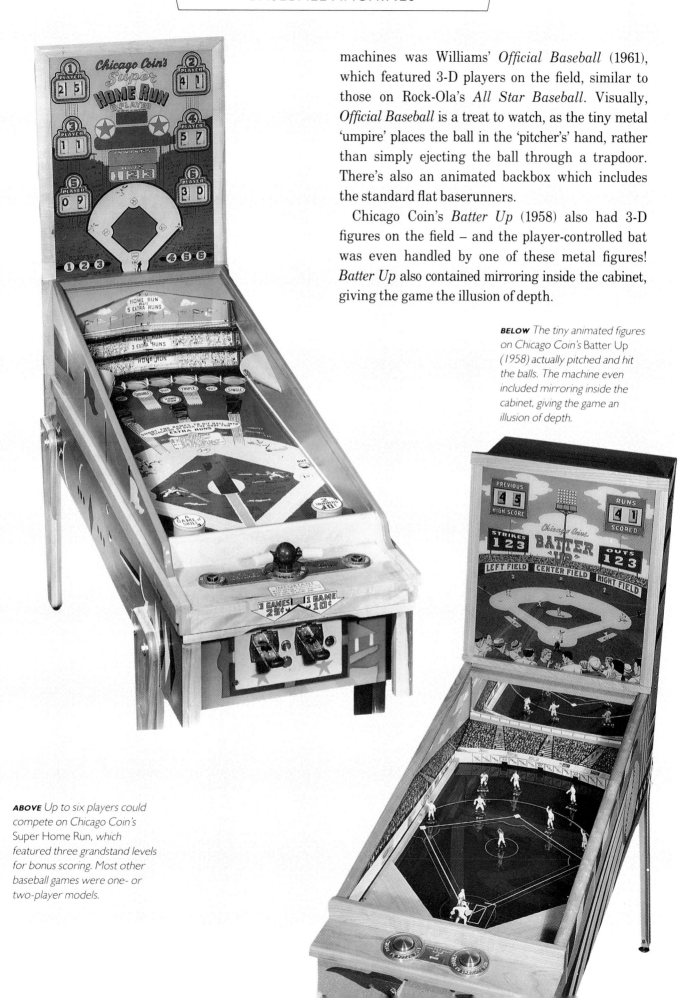

machines was Williams' *Official Baseball* (1961), which featured 3-D players on the field, similar to those on Rock-Ola's *All Star Baseball*. Visually, *Official Baseball* is a treat to watch, as the tiny metal 'umpire' places the ball in the 'pitcher's' hand, rather than simply ejecting the ball through a trapdoor. There's also an animated backbox which includes the standard flat baserunners.

Chicago Coin's *Batter Up* (1958) also had 3-D figures on the field – and the player-controlled bat was even handled by one of these metal figures! *Batter Up* also contained mirroring inside the cabinet, giving the game the illusion of depth.

BELOW *The tiny animated figures on Chicago Coin's* Batter Up *(1958) actually pitched and hit the balls. The machine even included mirroring inside the cabinet, giving the game an illusion of depth.*

ABOVE *Up to six players could compete on Chicago Coin's* Super Home Run, *which featured three grandstand levels for bonus scoring. Most other baseball games were one- or two-player models.*

Most of the post-war baseball machines could award replays just like pinball machines. And just as add-a-ball pinballs were created to avoid legal problems associated with awarding free games, baseball machines were also offered in extended play models, beginning in the early sixties.

The first of these was Williams' *Extra Inning* (1962), based on the company's 1962 *World Series*. Players could win up to nine extra innings by hitting grand slams, landing the ball in the 'Super Home Run' hole, getting home runs and for high scores. Interestingly, because you could win several extra innings on each game, the 'extended play' award was sometimes just as good as a free game, and sometimes better.

In the 1960s, Midway Manufacturing produced several baseball games which had unusual scoring systems. Unlike other baseball machines, Midway's games scored only runs, rather than singles, doubles and triples. While these games were decorated with baseball artwork, the play action had nothing to do with the theme.

For instance, instead of playing until three outs were registered, Midway's *Play Ball* (1965) gave players a predetermined number of pitches, usually between 25 and 50, depending on how the game was set. Playfield targets were worth up to ten runs, so it wasn't too difficult to accumulate scores of several hundred points.

Williams also produced some unconventional games in the late 1960s and early 1970s, such as *Fast Ball* (1969), which had an extra-wide playfield. More unusual was *Hit and Run* (1970). This game had no targets or scoring pockets; instead, there were several horseshoe-shaped metal guide rails on the field. A series of lights arranged in a square in the centre of the playfield represented a baseball diamond, and the object was to hit the ball as far toward the top of the field as possible, while the batter (indicated by a flashing light on the baseball diamond) ran as far around the diamond as he could before the ball rolled back to the bottom of the playfield. The game wasn't particularly popular, and the following year, Williams produced the more traditional–and popular–*Action Baseball*.

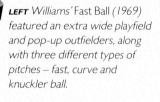

LEFT *Williams' Fast Ball (1969) featured an extra wide playfield and pop-up outfielders, along with three different types of pitches – fast, curve and knuckler ball.*

LEFT Line Drive (1972) was one of the last mechanical baseball machines produced by Williams Electronics. The game featured backbox animation, variable-speed pitching control and eight-track sound.

BELOW Williams' Pennant Fever (1984), designed by Mark Ritchie, was the first electronic baseball machine. It has proved so popular that Williams plans to release another baseball machine called Slugfest at the end of 1991.

In 1972, Williams introduced *Line Drive*, which featured eight-track sound. An 'announcer' narrated the game, while explosions and sirens would be heard during high scoring games. Williams' *Upper Deck* (1973) also included eight-track sound, and the playfield even featured an extra deck of targets. But the popularity of baseball machines had started to fade, and *Upper Deck* marked the end of production.

Williams revived coin-op baseball in 1984 with *Pennant Fever*. Designed by Mark Ritchie (and loosely based on *Action Baseball*), *Pennant Fever* featured a three-pitch selection and solid state sound, including an umpire's voice calling the strikes and outs. It was also the first (and only) baseball machine ever produced with digital scoring. Williams described the game: 'From *Take Me out to the Ball Game* to umpire calls and boos and cheers from the crowd, *Pennant Fever* brings the game alive.' Although *Pennant Fever* was popular with older players who enjoyed playing mechanical baseball machines, it never caught on with teenagers, the target group.

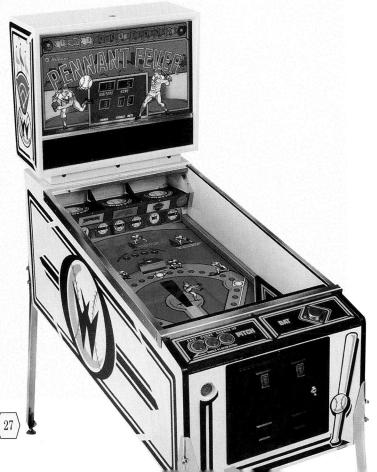

Several different styles of baseball machines have been produced. While all of them have used a pitch-and-bat type format, some – such as Keeney's *League Leader* (1958) – were very unusual. *League Leader* had several vertical decks or targets, with the lowest deck (at the playfield level) registering an out and the highest scoring a home run, with singles, doubles and triples in between. Other similar games have also appeared, including Bally's *Big Bat* (1984), Irving Kaye's *Batting Practice* (1965) and Munves' *Bat-a-Ball*, produced in the 1970s.

Chicago Coin produced an unusual line of upright baseball machines in the 1970s. *Baseball Champ* (1973), World Series (1974) and *Big League* (1975) were housed in vertical video-style cabinets. Players could select from three types of pitches, and aim at seven targets on the playfield, along with five bleacher and scoreboard targets. Chicago Coin packed quite a few features into these compact games, which play surprisingly well given their reduced playfield size.

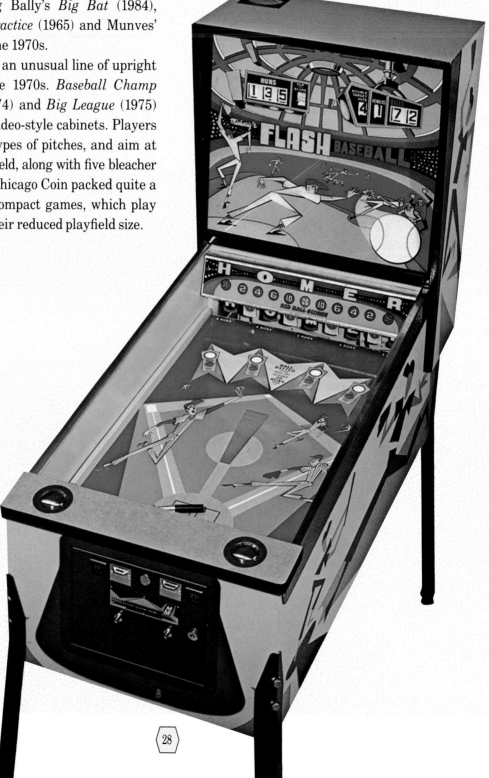

BELOW *Midway Manufacturing built several baseball machines in the 1960s, including* Flash Baseball *(1967). Although these games had a pitch-and-bat design and featured baseball artwork, they gave you a predetermined number of pitches, rather than registering strikes, hits and outs.*

Although baseball machines were always popular in the United States (especially during the 1950s and early 1960s), they were virtually unknown in the rest of the world, where sports such as soccer are far more popular than baseball. However, one of the few foreign countries to welcome baseball machines was Japan, where the sport is widely followed. In fact, two Japanese game manufacturers even produced their own baseball machines in the early 1970s.

Although most baseball machines offered essentially the same game, manufacturers had to come up with original baseball-related names for each new model. Some of the more interesting names include Williams' *King of Swat* (1955), Williams' *Four Bagger* (1956), Chicago Coin's *TV Baseball* (1966) and Scientific's *Pitch 'em & Bat 'em*, produced in the mid forties.

Baseball machines are sometimes referred to by the more generic name 'pitch and bat' games. While most pitch and bat machines had baseball themes, a few featured other motifs including football, golf and auto racing; these games are discussed elsewhere in the book.

Baseball machines, unlike other coin-op games, are seasonal. Some game operators would set them up for players in the spring, and put them into storage in the fall after the World Series. Some baseball machines were kept in service for ten to 15 years or more – much longer than most other coin-op games, which are usually in active service for about five to eight years.

Baseball games were always steady, dependable earners for operators. They appealed to players of all ages, from the youngsters who frequent arcades, to the blue-collar crowd that stops into the neighbourhood bar for a beer after work. Although these machines may be a little unsophisticated for some of today's younger players who grew up on fast-action video games, they still hold their nostalgic appeal for older players.

You can still find some baseball machines if you look around. Many are in seasonal resort arcades where the summer tourists love them. However, all

ABOVE *Players and collectors have always preferred the baseball machines manufactured by Williams Electronics, such as* Major League *(1963), which awarded free games and extra innings for 'over the fence' home runs.*

of these machines are over 15 years old, and as replacement parts become more difficult to obtain, these games are likely to disappear.

Among collectors, coin-operated baseball machines (especially those manufactured by Williams) are in great demand, particularly the games manufactured in the late 1950s and early 1960s which included backbox animation.

Playing a baseball machine can be very relaxing, because you can operate the game at your own pace; you can rest between pitches or take a break to plan your strategy, a luxury that you don't have on some coin-op games, particularly videos. Because there's an element of luck involved, every game is different – you can never truly master a baseball machine.

ARCADES AND THE LAW

To some politicians and law enforcement officials, arcade machines aren't simply amusement games — they're gambling devices designed to swindle unsuspecting victims.

Since the thirties, arcade machines have been taxed, banned, mutilated — and even destroyed — because uninformed lawmakers couldn't tell the difference between games of skill and gambling devices. Some local ordinances and regulations have imposed strict (and in some cases, laughable) restrictions on the games and their owners.

★ Because some of the games built in the 1930s and 1940s paid out cash or prizes, all coin-op machines were banned as gambling devices in many American cities. New York City Mayor, Fiorello LaGuardia, personally used a sledgehammer to destroy several pinball machines in the early forties. Rumours began circulating around this time that 'the mob' controlled all coin-op games; these rumours persist in some areas even today.

★ To silence critics who charged that replays (free games) were 'something of value' and thus qualified pinball machines as gambling devices, Gottlieb introduced *Flipper* in 1960. Instead of awarding replays, *Flipper* extended the length of your game by rewarding you with extra balls — up to ten, in some cases. Add-a-ball games like *Flipper* were operated in states like New York and Wisconsin, where replays were prohibited.

★ Although there were generally fewer restrictions on amusement games in Europe than in the US, Italy had very strict laws that banned free games. In fact, special pinball machines were produced exclusively for the Italian market in the 1960s and 1970s, because extra balls had to be shot from the outhole — between the flippers — rather than using the plunger.

★ In the mid 1970s, the sheriff of a rural southwestern Ohio county banned all pinball machines in his jurisdiction from awarding replays or extra balls. Pinball operators had to paint over the words 'Special When Lit' and 'Extra Ball When Lit' wherever they appeared on the games, and even had to cover the credit window in the backglass. And if the machine had

a free ball return gate, it had to be nailed shut!

★ Many communities passed anti-game legislation in the early eighties when video games grabbed the spotlight. Worried parents, who feared their children would become hopelessly addicted to the games, pushed for laws to prohibit children under 18 from playing amusement games during certain hours. Some cities limited the number of machines allowed in a location to one or two, while the games were completely banned in other towns. And a number of cities imposed amusement taxes of up to $2,000 (£1,000) per machine — per year — to discourage operators from opening arcades.

LEFT *United's* Tropicana, *a typical bingo machine from the 1950s. Although bingos may appear to resemble pinball machines, these games have no flippers and were banned as gambling devices in many cities, because they could award up to 999 free games.*

CHAPTER 3
Gun Games

Players have been enjoying the challenges offered by coin-operated gun and rifle games for more than six decades. These machines have appeared in several sizes and shapes, from compact table-top models to large games requiring more than 20 feet of floor space. Sadly, these mechanical shooting galleries are nearly extinct today, but if you're over 30, you'll probably remember playing them in penny arcades.

Coin-operated gun games have been around since the 1920s. The earliest models were completely mechanical and non-electric, with players firing tiny metal pellets at a variety of targets. When coin-op games began using electricity in the early thirties, players turned their attention to pinball and other arcade machines which featured more electrical action than gun games.

RIGHT *With World War II on the horizon, shooting games like Evans' Tommy Gun were among the most popular coin-op machines around in the late thirties and early forties.*

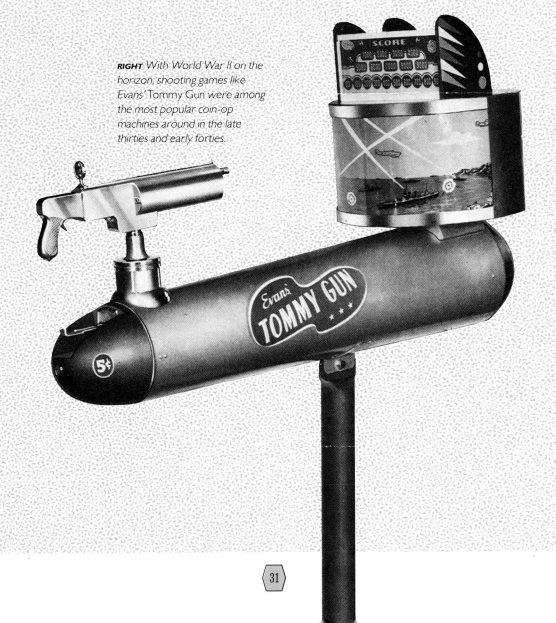

As the decade was drawing to a close, rifle game manufacturers added the latest electronic technology to their machines and attracted a new generation of players. In 1939, Seeburg introduced its *Multi-Rayolite Rifle Range,* one of the first shooting games to use photo-electric cells as 'targets'. This game had a full-scale replica rifle attached by a steel cable to a pedestal, with a separate 'target box' placed about ten to 15 feet away. The rifle fired a light beam at the moving targets, and the game registered 'hits' and 'misses'. This and other similar rifle games were often called 'ray guns' because they fired rays of light. Ray guns were an instant hit because the 'modern' technology was so different from the old-style mechanical gun games of only a few years earlier.

In the early 1940s, players eagerly dropped their coins into war-themed games like Keeney's *Submarine* and Evans' *Tommy Gun.* These machines featured moving targets (including submarines that bobbed up and down) and appealed to players' wartime patriotism. Keeney's *Anti-Aircraft Machine Gun,* for instance, featured a replica of a military anti-aircraft gun, complete with sight scope and handgrips. Players shot at moving aircraft projected on a screen 12 to 15 feet away. The planes would travel on different courses for each game, with over 3,000 different variations to keep players interested. The game even included flashing bursts of light from the gun barrel for an added touch of realism. At a nickel a play, *Anti-Aircraft Machine Gun* offered a welcome release from the realities of war.

Some ray-gun games were modified during the war to reflect the nation's patriotism. Mutoscope's *Shoot the Bartender,* which featured a moving mechanical bartender, was one of the most popular pre-war ray-gun rifle games. During the war, many operators purchased kits that transformed the barman into Hitler, Mussolini or Tojo. Nowadays, these wartime conversions are in great demand because of their historical significance.

After the war, gun games remained among the most popular coin-op devices. *Target Master* (1949), manufactured by Automatic Devices, Inc., was a small, two-piece unit designed to take up less than one square foot of space on a bar, counter or wall. *Target Master,* which featured a finely detailed gun that the company called 'an exact duplicate' of an army .45, was marketed towards locations which catered to war veterans, such as bars, barber shops and tobacconists. Arguably, the success of gun and rifle games in the post-war years was in any case due to the general public's fascination with US military derring-do in Europe and the Pacific.

The most famous rifle game of the 1950s is Seeburg's *Shoot the Bear* (1950). The game was simple; you shot the full-sized photo-electric rifle at a mechanical bear that moved from side to side in a target box ten feet away. If you hit the pacing bear in the chest, it would stand on its hind legs and growl, while a red light flashed in its mouth. A large part of *Shoot the Bear*'s appeal was its nostalgic, homespun humour. 'The bear is the target,' read the company's promotional material, 'but the hilarious antics of the dog get the laughs. When the bear is on the run, the dog is bold as brass – but watch him turn tail and "kite it" when the bear turns.'

Although only about 2,500 *Shoot the Bear* games were produced, its mechanical innovations, sound effects and attractive design, as well as its corny sense of humour, made it one of the most memorable rifle games. Seeburg also produced a few other ray gun-style rifle games in the fifties, including *Coon Hunt* and *Shoot the Chute.*

Dale Engineering's *Dale Burp Gun* was one of the more creative shooting games of the fifties. Players operated a machine gun, aiming at the masked gangsters that appeared randomly in the windows of the 'Crook's Saloon', a target box positioned 2½ feet away from the gun.

In the early 1950s, most game manufacturers replaced the large, two-piece rifle games with more compact one-piece models. Companies like Genco, Keeney, Exhibit, Williams and United produced these vertically styled machines which featured everything from small handguns to large rifles mounted at eye-level on a rotating base.

LEFT *Seeburg's Coon Hunt, produced in the early fifties, let you shoot a light beam at a photo-sensitive target box a few feet away. This machine is one of the most sought-after rifle games among collectors today, because of its humorous theme and unique sound effects.*

RIGHT *Many rifle games tried to capture all the fun of a carnival shooting-gallery, with moving rabbits, ducks and other revolving targets to test your marksmanship.*

Many gun games of the fifties had carnival or circus themes, such as United's *Carnival Gun* (1954) and Genco's *Big Top* (1954), *Circus* (1957) and *State Fair* (1956). By the end of the decade, America's fascination with the newly launched space program was reflected in games like Bally's *Space Gunner* (1958) and *Moon Raider* (1959).

But the most consistently popular theme for gun games was always the old West. Genco's *Wild West* (1958), Bally's *Gunsmoke* (1959) and Chicago Coin's *Pony Express* (1962) were just a few of the machines to use this motif.

Genco's *Davy Crockett* (1956) was based on the hit TV series, and was targeted specifically at the show's

LEFT *Genco was the leading manufacturer of gun games throughout the 1950s. Its* Rifle Gallery *rated your skill from 'Rifleman' and 'Marksman' to 'Sharpshooter' and 'Expert'.*

young viewers. *Davy Crockett* was designed especially for six-to-16-year-olds, according to Genco, and included a scaled-down cabinet with an attached pull-out step for small children.

Many of Genco's other rifle games simulated carnival shooting galleries. One of the most popular was *Gun Club* (1958), which included five clay pipes on a slowly turning wheel, running rabbits on an endless chain, foxes, flying ducks and even lighted candles that snuffed out when hit.

Williams produced several very unusual rifle games in the late 1950s. Rather than having the usual targets found on most rifle games, *Vanguard* (1958) had a square, 25-hole grid, with six or seven

BELOW *Exhibit's Dale Jet Gun (1954) featured rapid-fire* *machine-gun action set in an aerial gunfight.*

BELOW Exhibit's Dale Jet Gun (1954) featured rapid-fire machine-gun action set in an aerial gunfight.

shooting at selected targets to relaunch all or some of the balls. Williams released three more 'bouncing balls' rifle games – *Hercules* (1959), *Crusader* (1959) and *Titan* (1959). These bouncing ball games were unusual because they didn't test players' marksmanship; instead, high scores were achieved primarily by luck (after all, the bouncing *was* random), along with the strategy of deciding which balls to launch with each shot.

Bally also produced a bouncing-ball gun game. *Bally Derby* (1960) was a combination shooting/horse race game. Instead of scoring points, the bouncing balls would move five animated horses along a track, with players 'betting' on the winner.

Midway Manufacturing produced several unusual gun games in the early 1960s – unusual because they actually fired $^{11}/_{16}$-inch plastic balls at the targets rather than using photo-electric cells. *Shooting Gallery* (1960) and *Rifle Gallery* (1961) both featured large, plexiglass-enclosed target areas with moving and stationary targets. Bally's *Sharpshooter* (1961) and *Marksman* (1962) used the same principle, and Midway revived the concept with *White Lightning* (1970).

Chicago Coin produced two more ray gun-style rifles in the early 1960s. *Ray Gun* (1960) and *Wild West* (1961) were popular with players who had never seen these large, two-piece games before.

Throughout most of the 1960s and 1970s, only Williams, Midway and Chicago Coin produced mechanical rifle games. While Williams and Midway produced rather traditional pieces, Chicago Coin introduced several machine gun-style games, like *Texas Ranger* (1964). These games, which resembled telescopes, had two hand grips, with thumb-controlled firing buttons and mirrors inside the cabinets which created a 3-D effect – the targets seemed to be eight feet away!

Chicago Coin's *Champion Rifle* (1962) actually had a pinball game inside the cabinet. The pinball field had five kick-out holes and several rebound kickers; players aimed for the slowly moving pinball and the bullseyes in the centre of the playfield.

rubber balls inside. The grid was actually set horizontally inside the cabinet, but was reflected vertically in front of the rifle. At the start of the game, all of the balls would be launched and then land randomly in the holes; getting three or four balls in a row – or landing in the four corners – scored points. You then had 15 or 20 shots to score even more by

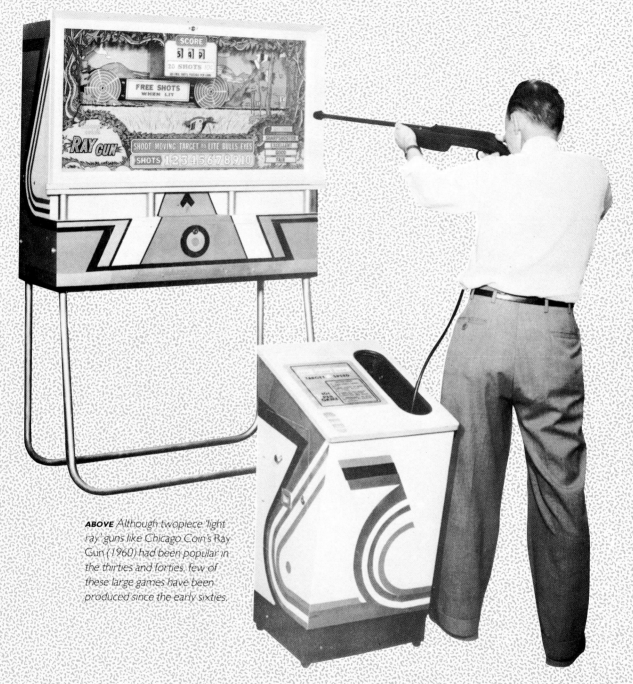

ABOVE *Although two-piece 'light ray' guns like Chicago Coin's Ray Gun (1960) had been popular in the thirties and forties, few of these large games have been produced since the early sixties.*

Rifle games began using black lighting for special effects in the early 1960s. The lighting created an optical illusion of depth, and made players feel that they were shooting at targets that were far off, rather than only a few inches away from them.

Eight-track sound also added a new dimension to rifle games. Midway's *One Million BC* (1969) had a prehistoric theme and soundtrack to match, as dinosaurs could be heard to roar during the game.

From the 1930s through the 1960s, most rifle games gave you a specific number of shots per game – often 20 or 25. However, by the end of the 1960s, most machines gave a predetermined amount of game time and an unlimited number of shots. This made the game a bit harder to play, because you could no longer casually line up your shots. Good players preferred this format because it rewarded their skill with higher scores.

In the early 1970s, mechanical rifle games fell into a rather predictable pattern. Most offered about eight to ten stationary and moving targets, included solid-state sound and used black lighting for special effects. Western themes were common, with games like Williams' *Stockade* (1975), Midway's *Top Gun* (1975) and Chicago Coin's *Shoot Out* (1976). Hunting was another popular motif, used on such games as Midway's *Wild Kingdom* (1972) and Chicago Coin's *Flying Ducks* (1973).

In the early 1970s, Nintendo produced one of the most unusual shooting games, *Wild Gunman*. This game used actual film footage of western outlaws projected on a large screen. You used a small handgun to outdraw the villains; if you were quicker than your opponent, the next gunman would appear, with up to five shoot-outs per game. Getting outdrawn by the gunman would end the game, though, and many first-time players were disappointed to find their game was over after only a few seconds.

LEFT *Chicago Coin's* Shoot Out *(1976) was one of the last electromechanical rifle games produced in the US, as video gun games began replacing traditional mechanical target galleries.*

The Stripper, which features a scantily clad western showgirl. You get five shots per game; each bullseye removes one of the five pieces of *The Stripper*'s clothing, with a perfect game revealing everything! Produced by a British company called Electrotechnics, *The Stripper* was too suggestive for many US arcades.

Mechanical rifle games were among the first machines to fall victim to video games. Even though video gun games couldn't offer the illusion of depth that mechanical rifle games could, they were able to speed up or slow down the action at random, change background settings and even picture moving targets from changing perspectives and angles.

Only a few video gun games have tried to simulate the look and feel of mechanical rifle games. Midway's *Desert Gun* (1975) and Stern's *Great Guns* (1980) were similar to traditional rifle games, with the mechanical targets replaced by video screens. Probably the most unusual video rifle game was Williams' *Turkey Shoot* (1984), which had 'real' turkey feathers flying around inside the cabinet!

The only true mechanical gun game produced in the eighties was Bally's *Midnight Marauders* (1984), which used mechanically operated moving targets rather than a video screen. Although this outer space-themed game included 3-D lighting effects, electronic sounds and even speech, it was largely overlooked by players.

Most gun games were designed for teenagers and middle-class white-collar workers. These players were often intrigued by the idea of shooting a gun, since most had probably never fired a real one. Rifle games were usually found in arcades, bowling alleys and discount stores, rather than blue-collar bars.

Unlike some coin-op machines, rifle games are 100 per cent skill games. Although some targets may pop up unexpectedly, their appearances are never completely random, and a good marksman should with practice be able to rack up high scores every time. The moving targets on many rifle games are controlled by a series of gears and pulleys attached to nylon fishing line, so you can anticipate the appearance of these targets after playing several games.

ABOVE *Most of the major game manufacturers introduced one new rifle game each year during the 1960s and seventies;* *Williams' entry for 1969 was Aqua Gun, which used black lighting to create a spectacular underwater effect.*

Several manufacturers have produced 'fast draw' gun games which let you go face-to-face with a life-sized cowboy mannikin to see who could draw faster. These mechanical outlaws taunted players with comments like 'Greenhorn – you couldn't hit the side of a barn!' and other insulting remarks.

The latest rifle game to use a life-sized mannikin is

Rifle games have often been targets for vandals, who removed the gun stocks from the machines; in some cases, the thieves converted them into home-made zip guns! By the 1970s, most rifle games had the stocks firmly anchored to the cabinets to discourage vandalism.

The days of mechanical gun games are long gone, although you can still find a few of them in arcades. It's a shame, too, because today's players will never know the feeling of satisfaction you get when you hit a moving target and watch it drop out of sight while hearing the mechanical clink of the machine. You just don't get that feeling hitting two-dimensional images on a video screen. Although video games may offer more realistic and dramatic graphics, mechanical gun games have a more solid and substantial feel to them.

RIGHT *Allied Leisure Industries built several popular gun games during the seventies, including Clay Champ, which pitted two players against each other in a test of speed and marksmanship. The 3-D effect was very well done.*

A BIG NAME IN DESIGN

If you've been in an arcade in the last 50 years, chances are good that you've played at least a few of the machines that Steve Kordek has designed.

Kordek, now the head designer at Williams Electronics, started working on coin-op games in 1937 when he was hired by Genco to troubleshoot games on the assembly line. Kordek stayed at Genco until the company went out of business 21 years later, and after a short time with Bally, he moved to business giants Williams Electronics, where he's been employed for the last 30 years.

Kordek has worked on virtually every type of coin-op game ever produced. He's designed rifle games, bowling machines and novelty arcade games, although he admits to a special affection for pinball. He's designed over 100 pinball machines, including Genco's *Triple Action* (1949), the first game with only two flippers. Some of the games that he created for Williams in the 1960s and 1970s are *Whoopee* (1964) which featured five captive balls 'trapped' in the centre

of the playfield; *Zodiac* (1971), a wide-body game with a centre ball shooter, and *Grand Prix* (1976) which had two separate bonus sytems.

One of Kordek's most popular machines (and one of his personal favourites as well) is *Space Mission* (1976), which featured a swinging target in the centre of the playfield. *Space Mission* pictured the Apollo link-up with the Soviet Soyuz spacecraft, and Kordek spent several days at NASA to learn about the project before he designed the game.

Today, Kordek supervises several designers working on Williams and Bally pinball machines, adding his own personal touches to each new game. You can still find some of the playfield features that Kordek invented years ago on today's machines. And if you listen closely to Williams' *Comet* pinball, you can hear his voice chanting 'A Million!' throughout the game. After more than 50 years of working with coin-op machines, Steve Kordek continues to shape the future of arcade games in inimitable style.

CHAPTER 4
Bowling Machines

Many coin-operated games have been based on actual sports, but few arcade machines have come as close to simulating the real thing as bowling machines. For over half a century, bowling games have been entertaining players. Today, these machines can still be found in bars and taverns where they're used in organized league competition just like real bowling alleys.

Designed for the penny arcades of the 1930s, the earliest coin-op bowling machines were about the same size and shape as pinball games. You simply shot a small ball at the two-inch pins near the top of the glass-enclosed playfield. Some of these machines recorded strikes and spares like real bowling, while others reset all ten pins after each shot. Although these machines were briefly popular in the late thirties, the games couldn't come close to matching the feel of real bowling.

In 1947, Lyn Durant of United Manufacturing designed the first 'shuffle alley', and even he was surprised by its success. The game, called simply *Shuffle Alley*, didn't look anything like earlier coin-op bowling machines; it was almost ten feet long and two feet wide with a long, wooden play area. You slid a small, metal puck along the smooth, polished surface toward the pins at the opposite end. The ten

LEFT *The first shuffle bowling machines, introduced in the late forties, used a puck instead of a ball to simulate the game of ten-pin bowling.*

BELOW United's Bowling Alley, unveiled in 1956, was the first machine to use 3-inch (7.5-cm) plastic bowling balls rather than a small metal puck; up to six players could compete on this 14-foot-long (4.25m) game.

miniature pins were mounted on a small raised platform above the playing surface. As the puck slid over the tiny metal sensor tips protruding from the playfield, the machine kept track of the strikes and spares scored during the ten-frame game, with players striving for a perfect score of 300.

Shuffle Alley was the first bowling machine that truly tested your skill. You could shoot the puck as hard or soft as you wanted to, put 'side' on the puck or bank it off one of the side rails. Instead of releasing the ball by pressing a button, you were now personally involved and had control of the action.

Shuffle alleys were among the hottest games around, and every manufacturer wanted a piece of the action. Within a few months of *Shuffle Alley*'s release, Exhibit, Keeney, Bally, Evans and Chicago Coin all introduced shuffle bowling games. In fact, these machines became so popular that Exhibit even produced a kit to convert two-sided rebound shuffleboard machines into bowling games! Exhibit's *Bowl-a-Matic* (1949) was essentially a large scoreboard with tiny bowling pins and hidden scoring wires that clipped on to one end of a standard shuffleboard; since most coin-op shuffleboards were between 18 and 22 feet long, shuffle bowling conversion kits like *Bowl-a-Matic* demanded a lot of skill!

Subtle refinements were added to shuffle alleys in the early fifties. United's *Double Shuffle Alley* (1950) featured lighted pins that went on and off to correspond with game scoring, and two-, four- and six-player games became common.

One of the most dramatic changes, though, was in pin size and location. Instead of small two-inch pins mounted above the playfield, manufacturers began placing five-inch plastic pins at puck level. Evans' *Shuffle Ten Strike* (1949) was one of the first machines to use this arrangement and featured large wooden pins with rubber bands around the bottom.

Although bowling centres across the US were enjoying unprecedented popularity in the mid fifties, only United, Chicago Coin and Bally were still building shuffle alleys. To cash in on America's love of bowling, United introduced *Bowling Alley* in 1956.

This 14-foot bowling machine used a three-inch ball instead of a puck, and was really a scaled-down simulation of real bowling.

Ball bowling games were much larger and heavier than shuffle alleys, and couldn't fit in many locations. But players loved the bowling realism that they offered, so manufacturers sold extenders to increase the length of the lanes. Operators could add these four-foot extenders to make the games 18 or 22 feet long, or even longer!

Ball bowling games were phenomenally popular with players – so popular, in fact, that United designed *Bowl-a-Rama* (1959) especially for businessmen who wanted to open their own coin-operated bowling centres. 'Bowl-a-Rama Centers equipped with up to 20 units have already proved to be one of the most profitable investments in the field of entertainment,' according to the company. 'Now is the time to establish your *Bowl-a-Rama* Center, and start yourself on the road to permanent prosperity.' The idea never got off the ground, though. Bally revived the concept in the mid sixties as *Bally Bowl-Arena*, although it was no more successful than United's effort.

In the early fifties, bowling machine manufacturers began introducing novel scoring features on each new model to keep players interested. Along with regulation scoring, some machines offered unusual twists like double- and triple-scoring strikes in selected frames. United's *Lightning* shuffle alley (1955) introduced Strike-A-Matic, which tested your accuracy along with your timing. *Lightning* awarded from 150 to 800 points for each strike, depending on the value that was indicated by a random, moving light when the strike was made, so that you had to time your shot carefully. This scoring system (also called Flash and Flash-O-Matic) became one of the most popular bowling machine features.

United's *Handicap* shuffle alley (1956) included an equalizing feature. At the start of the game, each player could select from 'easy' strikes (for 'average' bowlers), 'medium' strikes (for 'good' bowlers) or 'hard' strikes (for 'expert' bowlers). The machine could adjust the strike zone for different skill levels.

By the early sixties, players could pick from even more scoring options. United's *5-Way* shuffle alley (1961) let you select from 'regulation scoring', 'all strikes' (with strikes scoring 300), 'progressive scoring' (with consecutive strike and spare values increasing), 'advance scoring' (with strike and spare

values automatically increasing throughout the game) and 'all spares' (with spares scoring 300).

In the late 1950s and early 1960s, United produced a few small ball bowling machines. Called 'roll down' bowlers, *Midget Alley* (1958), *Pixie Bowler* (1958), *Silver* (1961) and *Circus* (1962) were about the size of shuffle alleys, but used three-inch balls instead of pucks. The games featured several different scoring options, but never caught on.

With the introduction of *Shuffle Alley* in 1947, United became the leading manufacturer of bowling machines, a position it held throughout the 1950s and early sixties (although the company also produced several other less successful types of coin-op games). After Williams Electronics purchased United in 1964, Williams kept the United name on its bowling machines for more than two decades because of United's reputation for good-quality products.

Like other coin-op games, bowling machines reflected popular culture. One of the most unusual games was Midway's *Fantastic* shuffle (1968), which featured day-glo pink and green pins and 'swinging hippie colors', according to the company. But national interest in bowling dropped during the

ABOVE *Most shuffle alleys let you select one of several scoring variations. United's Gamma (1968) offered you a choice of 'Flash' and 'Strike-O-Matic', in addition to regulation scoring.*

1960s, and so did players' interest in bowling machines. Ball bowlers were particularly hard hit, because they were so large and so expensive; a new ball bowling game cost operators more than twice as much as a new pinball machine.

The introduction of video games in the early seventies led to the demise of ball bowling machines because of limited production space and ball bowlers' sagging sales. Williams' *El Grande* (1973) and Chicago Coin's *Gold Medal* (1975) marked the end of mechanical ball bowler production. Both Williams and Chicago Coin continued to produce shuffle alleys, though. Williams' *Topaz* (1978) introduced digital

scoring on shuffle alleys, and brought the games into the electronic era.

Shuffle alleys sold very poorly in the early 1980s. In fact, between 1980 and 1984, only three new versions were produced, all by Williams – *Taurus* (1980), *King Tut* (1981) and *Omni* (1982).

When the video game boom went bust in the mid 1980s, many game operators returned to the old stand-by of bowling machines. US Billiards, a leading pool table manufacturer, introduced *Super-Bowl* (1983), a 14-foot ball bowler. Like earlier mechanical bowling machines, *Super-Bowl* could be expanded to up to 30 feet through extender sections. Also, players could select from six different games, including 'Regulation', 'Flash-O-Matic' and 'Red Strike'. *Super-Bowl* also included a 25-inch colour screen over the pins to attract video game players. Not only that, but players received a printed ticket at the end of the game with frame-by-frame scoring information.

The following year, Bally introduced *10 Pin Deluxe*, the first shuffle alley with a video screen instead of moving pins. The game featured 3-D pins projected on the screen and video 'cartoons' between frames. Bowling purists didn't like the modern look of the machine and the game was too slow and passive for younger video game players.

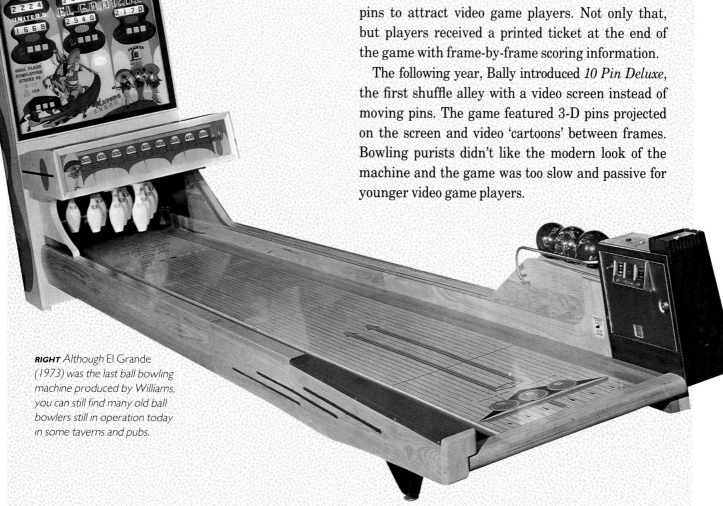

RIGHT *Although* El Grande *(1973) was the last ball bowling machine produced by Williams, you can still find many old ball bowlers still in operation today in some taverns and pubs.*

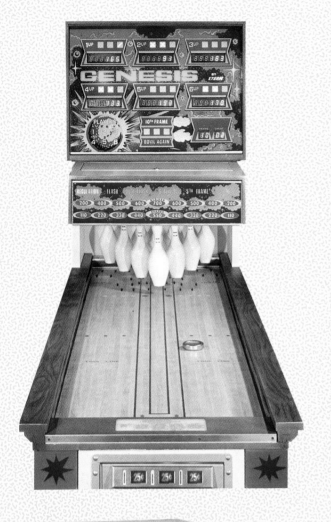

In the last few years, though, traditional shuffle alleys have made a minor comeback. Since 1984, Williams has introduced one or two new games per year, including *Triple Strike* (1984), *Gold Mine* (1987) and *Shuffle Inn* (1989). Williams' *Alley Cats* (1985) is one of the most creative shuffle alleys, and features ten 'beer bottles' rather than pins. The sound of shattering glass is heard when strikes are scored.

If you've ventured into any blue-collar bars recently, you probably found a bowling machine there. Game operators report that bowling machines have been bringing in steady revenue in the last few years, in part because tournaments and bowling leagues have been organized around the games. Some operators have even supplied large scoreboards and trophies to encourage player participation.

Even though the last ball bowling machines were produced more than 15 years ago, a surprising number of them (including some from the fifties) are still earning money today. The biggest problem that operators have with these old games is finding replacement parts!

Very few game collectors are interested in bowling machines, particularly the ball bowlers. Although the names may be different, all of these machines offer essentially the same game. Not only that, but the artwork on the machines is generally unattractive, especially on those produced in the 1960s and 1970s But most of all, they're heavy! The average shuffle alley weighs at least 450 lb (200 kg), while most ball bowlers tip the scale at 900 lb (400 kg)!

LEFT With their bland artwork, many of the bowling machines built in the early seventies are considered to be among the least attractive coin-op games ever produced. The art on Chicago Coin's Caprice (1971) is typical of this style.

TOP LEFT Genesis (1978) was the first of only two shuffle bowling games produced by Stern Electronics, formerly known as Chicago Coin. By the late 1970s, the demand for these games had dropped so much that Williams Electronics was the only manufacturer still producing bowling machines.

It's unlikely that coin-operated bowling machines will ever regain the popularity that they enjoyed in the 1950s and early sixties, when more than 125 different models were produced. Bowling machines are so bulky that they take up space that could be filled by other games. They therefore need to be played constantly to ensure a good profit for their owners. Also, today's younger generation of video players demands games that 'fight back' and get progressively more difficult, rather than 'passive' games like bowling machines.

Still, there's something wonderfully nostalgic about bowling machines. Maybe because their basic design hasn't changed in almost 40 years, they're still enjoyed by older players who never outgrew them.

ABOVE *Many game operators organize weekly leagues and tournaments around their shuffle alleys and even award plaques and trophies to the top players. Electronic bowling machines like Williams' Tic Tac Strike are ideally suited to these competitions.*

MANUFACTURERS AROUND THE WORLD

Despite the dominance of American manufacturers, coin-op games have been produced in several countries around the world. Here are some of these countries — and a few of the companies based there.

AUSTRALIA	Cashbox Amusement Company (Melbourne)
	Hankin (Newcastle)
FRANCE	Cifa (Copendu)
	Christian Tabart (Montgeron)
	Jeutel (Toucy)
	Rally (Nice)
	Réné Pierre (Ranchot)
	Sirica (Paris)
	Staal (Neuilly)
GERMANY	Bergmann (Rellingen)
	Forster (Furth)
	Geiger (Immenstadt)
	NSM (Bingen)
	Wulff (Hanover)
HOLLAND	Royal (Tilburg)
IRELAND	Silicon (Dublin)
ITALY	AMI (Torino)
	Bell Games (Bologna)
	BEM (Milan)
	CEA (Bologna)
	Elettrocoin (Firenze)
	IDI (Alessandria)
	Mister Game (Bologna)
	Nordamatic (Verona)
	Tecnoplay (San Marino)
	Zaccaria (Bologna)
	Zodiac (Firenze)
JAPAN	Capcom (Tokyo)
	Data East (Tokyo)
	Jaleco (Tokyo)
	Konami (Tokyo)
	Namco (Tokyo)
	Sega (Tokyo)
	Taito (Tokyo)
	Universal (Tokyo)
SPAIN	Automaticos Montecarlo (Madrid)
	Bill Port (Madrid)
	Centro Matic (Madrid)
	Cirsa (Barcelona)
	Inder (Madrid)
	Interflip (Madrid)
	Jocmatic (Barcelona)
	MAC (Madrid)
	Playbar (Barcelona)
	Playmatic (Barcelona)
	Recel/Euro Flip/Juegos Populares (Madrid)
	Recreativos Franco (Madrid)
	Peyper (Madrid)
	Segasa/Sonic (Madrid)
SWITZERLAND	Padorex (Lausanne)

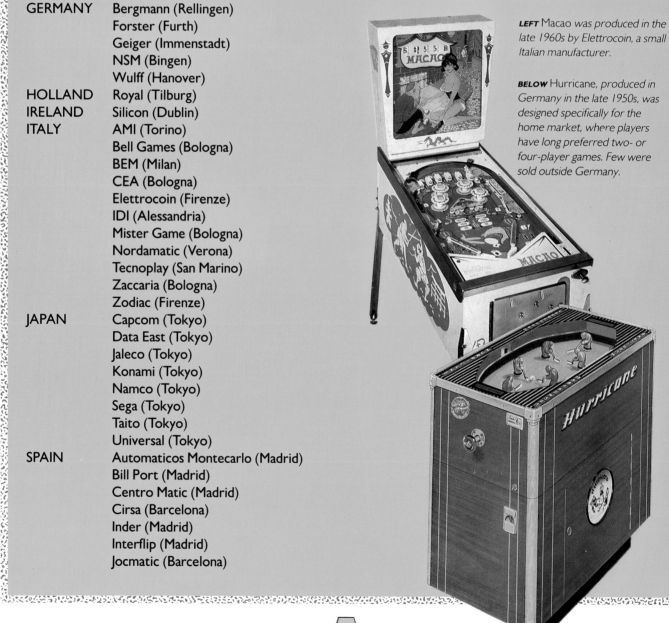

LEFT Macao was produced in the late 1960s by Elettrocoin, a small Italian manufacturer.

BELOW Hurricane, produced in Germany in the late 1950s, was designed specifically for the home market, where players have long preferred two- or four-player games. Few were sold outside Germany.

CHAPTER 5
Pinball Machines

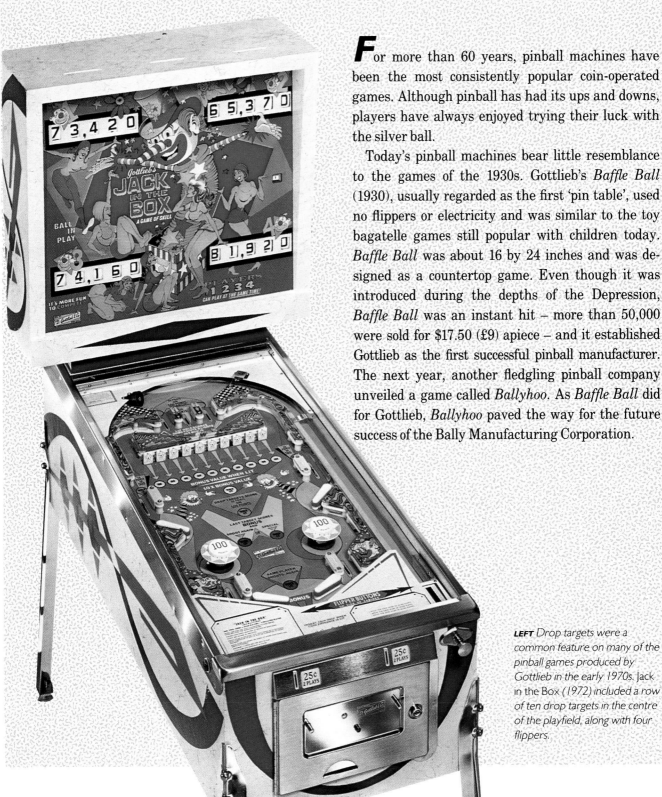

*F*or more than 60 years, pinball machines have been the most consistently popular coin-operated games. Although pinball has had its ups and downs, players have always enjoyed trying their luck with the silver ball.

Today's pinball machines bear little resemblance to the games of the 1930s. Gottlieb's *Baffle Ball* (1930), usually regarded as the first 'pin table', used no flippers or electricity and was similar to the toy bagatelle games still popular with children today. *Baffle Ball* was about 16 by 24 inches and was designed as a countertop game. Even though it was introduced during the depths of the Depression, *Baffle Ball* was an instant hit – more than 50,000 were sold for $17.50 (£9) apiece – and it established Gottlieb as the first successful pinball manufacturer. The next year, another fledgling pinball company unveiled a game called *Ballyhoo*. As *Baffle Ball* did for Gottlieb, *Ballyhoo* paved the way for the future success of the Bally Manufacturing Corporation.

LEFT *Drop targets were a common feature on many of the pinball games produced by Gottlieb in the early 1970s. Jack in the Box (1972) included a row of ten drop targets in the centre of the playfield, along with four flippers.*

RIGHT National Pin Games' The Pilot (1932) is typical of the bagatelle-style pinball machines produced in the early 1930s. These games used no electricity, had no flippers, and were usually small enough to fit on a small table or counter top.

These early games were rather crude by today's standards. After you shot the ball, you simply watched it roll slowly down the playfield into the scoring holes (small pockets surrounded by a ring of pins or nails, which is how pinball got its name). You even tabulated your own score on these early games! Still, pinball was incredibly popular, and during the thirties, more than 150 companies tried their luck at producing pingames, although only a handful of manufacturers remained by the end of the decade.

When electricity was added to pinball in the mid 1930s, the games took on a more modern appearance. Gone were the small counter-sized games, as back-boxes were added that automatically displayed your score. Bally's *Rockelite* (1936) was the first machine to include automatic scoring: its backglass had a series of numbers increasing in increments and illuminated by small lightbulbs behind the glass to keep track of the score.

One of the most familiar pinball devices was introduced on Bally's *Bumper* (1936). Before *Bumper* appeared, your score was determined entirely by the pockets into which the balls dropped. *Bumper* introduced bumpers – metal posts surrounded by coiled springs that scored points when touched by the ball. Bumpers wouldn't have been practical on pinball machines before electricity made automatic scoring possible, but they quickly became enormously popular with players. Most pinball machines of the late thirties and early forties included at least ten bumpers – and some had more than 20. Stoner's *Ali Baba* (1939), for instance, boasted a whopping 24 bumpers! Nearly every pinball machine produced since *Bumper* has included at least one or two bumpers on the playfield.

One of the most infamous pinball devices, the tilt, was also invented in the 1930s by Harry Williams, and first appeared on Bally's *Signal* (1934). Originally called a 'stool pigeon', this device was actually a small steel ball that rested atop a one-inch pedestal; if you shook the machine too hard, the ball would fall from the pedestal and land on a metal ring which would complete an electrical circuit and end the game.

Today's pinball machines use a small cone-shaped plumb bob suspended through a metal ring rather than a ball and pedestal. Some players still try to nudge the machine without activating the dreaded tilt mechanism, and consider 'body english' (as it is known) an integral part of the game.

Pinball had lost much of its lustre by the end of the decade, and production ceased completely in 1942 as the US economy shifted to wartime production. Gottlieb, Bally, Chicago Coin, Genco, Keeney and other manufacturers converted their assembly lines to produce such wartime products as machine gun parts, rocket components and parachute equipment.

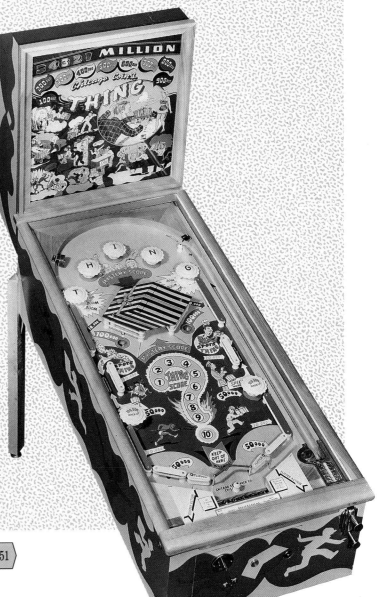

BELOW *Chicago Coin was best known for its novelty arcade games, although the company did produce many pinball machines including* The Thing *(1951), which featured a hidden bumper that awarded random 'mystery' scores.*

During the war, several small companies offered pinball conversion kits with names like *Smack the Japs* (1943) and *Victorious* (1944), but these conversions were little more than a new backglass and a few plastic playfield parts to update out-of-date pre-war games.

After the war, pinball manufacturers returned to 'business as usual'. Because game development had been put on hold during the war, most post-war machines resembled those that had been produced nearly a decade earlier, with simple arrangements of bumpers and rollover lanes. Players were looking for something new, and they got it in 1947.

A Gottlieb engineer named Harry Mabs was working on a baseball-style pitch-and-bat game (like those described in Chapter 2) when he accidentally activated the bat several times in succession, bypassing the machine's built-in delay system which normally prevented the bat from swinging more than once after each ball was released. Mabs applied this continuous bat action to pinball, and added several player-controlled bats to hit the ball *up* the playfield. Introduced in October 1947, *Humpty Dumpty* was the first game to include this new invention – flippers.

Humpty Dumpty sported three pairs of two-inch 'flipper bumpers', as they were originally called. Two flippers were placed at the bottom of the playfield, two near the middle and two at the top, so you could relay the ball up the entire playfield. For the first time, you could actively manipulate the ball, rather than just watch passively as it rolled down the field. Promotional material declared *Humpty Dumpty* to be 'The greatest triumph in pin game history! Phenomenal is the word for this play-inspiring Gottlieb innovation! Unique flipper bumpers are motivated by sensitive finger-tip control buttons on each side of the cabinet. With skill and timing, a player can control balls and send them zooming right back to the top of the playing field for additional scoring! The combination of controlled Flipper Button action and controlled ball action provides amazing earning power . . . a proven shot-in-the-arm for any location.'

Humpty Dumpty was an overnight sensation. By the end of 1947, pre-flipper pinball machines were obsolete, and every manufacturer had either produced its own flipper-equipped pinball or had one in development. Flipper retrofit kits were even available to add the devices to outdated pre-war machines.

Because of limitations in electrical current, the flippers on these early flipper games were very weak, in comparison to those on later games. The machines usually required six flippers to manoeuvre the ball all the way up the playfield. Genco designer Steven Kordek engineered stronger flippers on his company's games in the late forties, and created the first pinball machine with only two flippers; this design was quickly adopted by the other manufacturers. But by the mid 1950s, the novelty of flippers had worn off, and only Gottlieb and Williams Electronics (formed by designer Harry Williams in 1945) continued to produce pinballs.

Gottlieb quickly established itself as the 'king' of pinball in the 1950s. Games like *Knock Out* (1950), *Happy Days* (1952), *Mystic Marvel* (1954), *Gypsy Queen* (1954) and *Dragonette* (1954) helped make Gottlieb games of this decade the favourites of players. The company's card-themed games like *Queen of Hearts* (1952) and *Poker Face* (1953) were especially popular.

Since the 1930s, pinball had used light-up scoring on the backglass. A score of 2,560,000, for example, would be indicated by lightbulbs behind the glass illuminating a '2 million' panel, a '500,000' panel and a '60,000' panel. But scoring changed dramatically in the mid fifties when Gottlieb and Williams replaced the light-up scoring with score reels. These reels were actually rotating drums with '0' through '9' printed on them, and they kept score in much the same way as a car's odometer registers mileage.

Gottlieb's *Super Jumbo* (1954) was the company's first game with score reels – and the first pinball machine designed for more than one player. Until 1954, pinball was strictly a single-player game because the light-up scoring system was too cumbersome to keep track of more than one person's score at all easily. *Super Jumbo* was the first machine that catered for four players, and Gottlieb trumpeted their latest innovation with a new slogan to promote it: 'It's More Fun to Compete!'

The 1950s is sometimes called the 'golden age of pinball'. Although relatively few new playfield features were introduced during this decade, most of the games had simple-to-understand layouts with easily assimilated rules. Pinball was still relegated primarily to pool halls, bowling alleys, bars and other 'unsavoury' places, but the post-war baby boom generation was discovering the joy of flipper games. As Gottlieb declared on its machines of the fifties: 'Amusement Pinballs – As American As Baseball and Hot Dogs!'

LEFT *Steve Kordek designed Williams' Whoopee (1965), which featured five 'captive' balls in the centre of the playfield. The design was updated several years later and released as Jubilee (1973).*

Pinball machines were designed to play faster in the 1960s. They included stronger bumpers and flippers than earlier games, and the score reels could record the targets hit by a fast-moving ball more accurately than the old-style light-up backglass scoring could. Two- and four-player games were more common, and pinball became more respectable as the games began appearing in 'family' locations like discount stores and restaurants.

Pinball themes were more family-oriented in the sixties. Gottlieb's *Central Park* (1966), for instance, pictured a happy organ grinder and a playful monkey ringing a bell, which appealed to women and children, as well as the traditional male players. Of course,

RIGHT Gottlieb produced several machines with backbox animation in the 1960s. One of the most popular was Skyline (1965), which featured elevator doors that opened to reveal a comical scene.

many games featured outer space themes, with the US space program dominating the news. Williams' *Friendship 7* (1962) pictured astronaut John Glenn alongside his spacecraft.

In 1963, pinball experienced a surge in popularity, and several new (and old) makers unveiled flipper games. Bally, Chicago Coin and Keeney all re-entered the pinball arena after several years' absence, along with newcomer Midway Manufacturing.

Several games of the 1960s included backbox animation, with moving objects visible through a 'window' in the backglass. This animation was often predictable, such as a cannon that fired a small plastic ball whenever an extra ball was awarded on Gottlieb's *Flipper Parade* (1961).

But some of the best-loved games of the sixties featured comical animation designed to amuse and entertain players. You could tell that a gag would be revealed through the animation, but you had to play the game (or watch someone else play it) to learn the punchline. A classic example was Gottlieb's *Crosstown* (1966), which pictured a crowded subway car in a busy station; opening the car's animated doors revealed the conductor ejecting a tuba-carrying passenger from the car.

Other games featured backbox animation designed simply to catch your eye. Gottlieb's *Dodge City* (1964) included a dancing marionette-style cowboy with an uncanny resemblance to American TV favourite Howdy Doody, while Gottlieb's *Dancing Lady* (1967) featured a 3-D ballerina performing a pirouette. One of the most popular animated games was Gottlieb's *Buckaroo* (1965), in which a bucking bronco kicked a hapless cowboy in the behind.

In 1970, all of the pinball manufacturers replaced the standard two-inch flippers with longer three-inch flippers. These larger flippers, which are still used today, gave players more control over the ball and the games came to rely more on skill.

BELOW Williams' Suspense (1969) had an unusual playfield that included two sets of flippers and a mini roulette wheel in the centre of the playfield. The game's artwork captured the psychedelic atmosphere of the era.

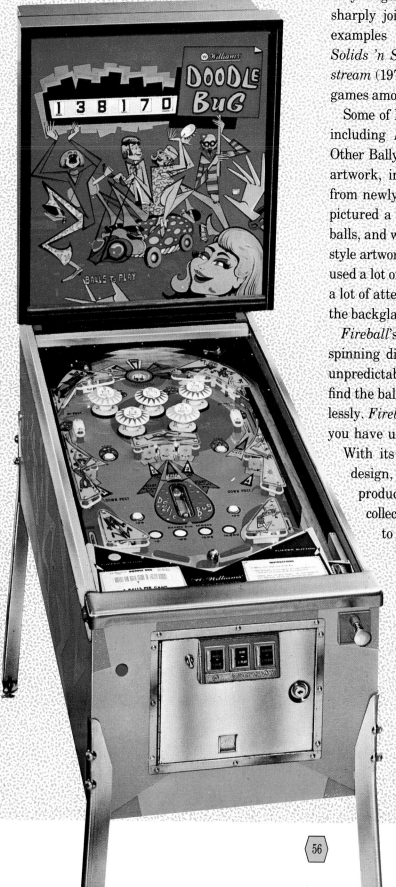

In the late 1960s, pinball artwork began to change, especially on Williams' games. The drawings became very angular and featured characters with long, sharply jointed arms and legs. Some outstanding examples of this artistic style include Williams' *Solids 'n Stripes* (1970), *Stardust* (1972) and *Gulfstream* (1973). Most pinball collectors consider these games among the least attractive ever produced.

Some of Bally's games also used this angular style, including *Firecracker* (1971) and *Mariner* (1971). Other Bally pinballs had more detailed contemporary artwork, including *Fireball* (1972), the first effort from newly hired artist Dave Christensen. *Fireball* pictured a mythical man-like monster hurling fireballs, and was a definite departure from the cartoon-style artwork found on most other games. Christensen used a lot of deep reds and blues on *Fireball* and paid a lot of attention to detail, on the playfield as well as the backglass.

Fireball's playfield was also unique. It featured a spinning disc which sent the ball rolling wildly in unpredictable directions; even the best player could find the ball flung out of play while he watched helplessly. *Fireball* was also a multiball game, which let you have up to three balls on the playfield at once.

With its dazzling artwork and unique playfield design, *Fireball* was an instant hit – 3,815 were produced – and the game is still popular among collectors today, often selling for $1,000 (£500) to $2,000 (£1,000) or more.

LEFT *The angular artistic style found on Williams' Doodle Bug (1971) was typical of the design found on many of the pinball games which were produced in the early seventies.*

Bally produced several other popular pinballs in the mid seventies, including *Flicker* (1975), which pictured Laurel and Hardy on the backglass, and *Air Aces* (1975) which included a row of nine drop targets in the centre of the playfield. Gottlieb's *Top Score* (1975) was a bowling-themed pinball with rolling plastic balls providing the backbox animation, and Williams' *Jubilee* (1973) featured five 'captive' pinballs on the playfield.

The 1975 movie *Tommy* helped to glorify and glamorize pinball, and also spawned two very popular machines based on the film, Bally's *Wizard* (1975) and *Captain Fantastic* (1976). Suddenly, everyone wanted to be a 'pinball wizard'. Players lined up in arcades to play games like Williams' *Space Mission*

(1976) and *Grand Prix* (1976), Gottlieb's *Spirit of 76* (1976) and *Royal Flush* (1976) and Bally's *Old Chicago* (1976).

Bally even held several national pinball tournaments in its Aladdin's Castle arcades, and found that many of the entrants were adults, and that they included doctors, lawyers and housewives. The old stereotype pinball player – a leather-jacketed thug smoking a cigarette – was replaced by a businessman in a three-piece suit.

Pinball manufacturers couldn't produce machines quickly enough to satisfy players, so a couple of European game companies began shipping their products to the US. A Spanish company called Sonic found success with games like *Prospector* (1976) and *Super Straight* (1977), while *New World* (1976) by Playmatic, another Spanish manufacturer, was also popular. Still, these European-built games didn't have the durability or long-term play appeal of American pinballs and were often merely copies of popular US games.

With pinball's popularity at an all-time high, industry leader Bally unveiled *Freedom* (1977), the first game from a major company with digital scoring. Although two small manufacturers had previously introduced digital pinball games, *Freedom* was the first machine to include all solid-state components, something that appealed to game operators. Williams and Gottlieb produced their own digital machines soon after – *Hot Tip* and *Cleopatra*, respectively.

LEFT *Bally's Flicker (1975) honoured movie legends including Laurel and Hardy, W. C. Fields and Clark Gable. The playfield featured two 'captive' balls and a single thumper bumper surrounded by a rebound ring.*

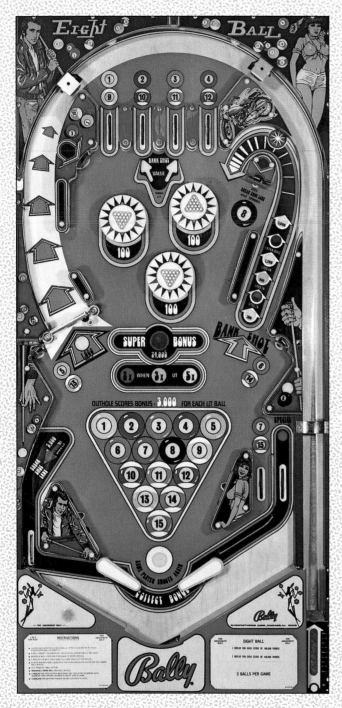

LEFT Eight Ball *(1977), which featured Fonzie from TV's* Happy Days, *was a big winner for Bally. Over 20,000 of these games were built, the largest production run of any flipper pinball machine, and a sign of the star's appeal.*

age of pinball's popularity by producing 'cocktail' pinballs. Game Plan and Allied Leisure Industries each produced about half a dozen of these small sit-down games. These compact machines were ideally suited for locations that either couldn't fit a standard pinball or whose owners didn't want one because of the noise and the 'gaudiness'.

Celebrity-themed pinballs were common in the late seventies, and Bally led the way with games like *Evel Knievel* (1977), *Playboy* (1978), *Star Trek* (1979), *Kiss* (1979) and *Dolly Parton* (1979). Gottlieb also had its share of celebrity games including *Close Encounters of the Third Kind* (1978), *Charlie's Angels* (1978) and *James Bond* (1980), while Stern Electronics produced *Ted Nugent* (1978) and *Muhammed Ali* (1980).

Artwork became more sophisticated on pinballs during this time. Bally's *Lost World* (1978) is considered an artistic masterpiece with its almost three-dimensional effect. *Lost World* is one of artist Paul Faris' favourite designs, as the mythical hero on the backglass is actually a self-portrait, while his wife served as the model for the woman seated beside him. *Lost World*'s art proved to be so popular with players that Faris used the characters again on Bally's *Paragon* (1979).

In 1978, the familiar pinball chimes were replaced with electronic organ tones and synthesized music. Williams' *Flash* (1978) combined a well-designed playfield and great artwork with a unique sound package that included high-intensity background tones, explosions and thunderclaps.

The following year, Williams produced a pinball landmark – *Gorgar*, the first talking pingame. With a menacing voice to match the monster on the backglass, *Gorgar* taunted players with phrases like 'Me Gorgar, Beat Me' and 'You Hurt Gorgar'. *Gorgar*'s pounding heartbeat could even be heard in the background. While *Gorgar*'s voice wasn't always audible

Bally's greatest success was *Eight Ball* (1977), which set a company production record of 20,230 games manufactured, a record that still stands today. *Eight Ball* pictured the leather-jacketed Fonzie character from TV's 'Happy Days' and had a 'memory' that could remember which targets had been hit on the previous ball.

Two small manufacturers decided to take advant-

in noisy arcades, sound had become an integral part of pinball's appeal.

Many new and unique game ideas were tried at this time. Bally's *Xenon* (1980) had a transparent tube that transported the ball from one side of the playfield to the other, while Williams' *Firepower* (1980) introduced multiball play on digital games. And Gottlieb's *James Bond* (1980) gave you 'time units' rather than a specified number of balls and you could win extra time units to extend the game.

LEFT *Midway's Gun Fight (1975) let you challenge another player to a wild west shoot-out, or take on the machine if you were playing alone; the game featured 'pistol grip' firing controls.*

Pinball's fortunes started to decline in 1980, as video games like Atari's *Asteroids*, Nintendo's *Donkey Kong* and Midway's *Pac Man* lured players away from the silver ball. Williams' *Black Knight* (1980) was the first double-level pinball machine, and although it included multiball play and a host of other new features, it still wasn't enough to recapture players' interest.

Some pinball manufacturers even followed the old adage, 'If you can't beat 'em, join 'em' and built combination pinball/video games. Gottlieb's *Caveman* (1982) had a standard-sized pinball playfield with a video game screen mounted in the centre, controlled by a joystick on the front of the cabinet. Bally also produced two pinball/video games – *Baby Pac Man*

(1982) and *Granny and the Gators* (1983), although none of these games met with success.

Pinball rebounded in the fall of 1984 when Williams unveiled *Space Shuttle*. The company had been hit hard by pinball's decline, and designer Barry Oursler included more new features on *Space Shuttle* than had been seen on any machine in years. The result was a masterpiece of a game, with two criss-cross ramps, excellent sound (including speech), multiball play and more. There was even a model of a space shuttle on the playfield! *Space Shuttle* was the most popular machine – pinball or video – at the national coin-op trade show that year.

The following year, Williams released *Comet*, which featured the first million-point shot in pinball. *High Speed* (1986) was another Williams hit. Designed by Steve Ritchie (who had also created *Flash, Firepower* and *Black Knight*), *High Speed* featured a police chase theme with a flashing red light atop the machine. *High Speed* boasted several innovations, including a 'jackpot bonus'; if you could make the difficult ramp shot during multiball play, you received a jackpot of up to 2 million points! Everyone loved *High Speed*, including many video players who hadn't touched a pinball machine in years. If an arcade had only one pinball, it was *High Speed*.

Williams' *Pinbot* (1986) was another hit and featured a row of disappearing targets at the top of the playfield. *Cyclone* (1988) was yet another popular Williams game which featured a moving ferris wheel that fitted in well with its amusement park theme. The pinball obituaries which had been written only three or four years earlier were forgotten, and pinball was back in the spotlight once again.

THE CREATIVE PROCESS

Creating a pinball machine is a long, complicated process that takes about a year and requires the talents of several specialists, including a game designer, mechanical engineer, programmer and artist. It costs almost a million dollars to produce a single finished prototype of a new game. Here's a quick look at some of the highlights in the creation of a machine.

The whole process starts with the game designer. He's the one who arranges the targets, bumpers, spinners and ramps on the playfield. A mechanical engineer builds new playfield features to the designer's specifications, and together they create a layout that combines skill shots with lucky bounces so that both novices and experts can enjoy the game.

Each game has its own unique set of rules; for example, hitting the drop targets may advance the bonus multiplier, or completing a sequence of rollover lanes may score an extra ball. A programmer encodes all of this information on to computer chips, along with all the sounds you hear during the game.

Next comes the 'whitewood' stage. A complete working model is built to test the machine's design; it's played over and over, hundreds of times, to make certain that there are no dead or inaccessible spots on the playfield. Moving a bumper even a fraction of an inch can affect the way the game plays, so every feature is scrutinized. Players time these test games to make sure the games don't last too long or end too quickly.

During these early stages, an artist will be creating the backglass illustration. Sometimes several different backglass drawings are made before one is selected for the game. After the backglass art is finished, work begins on the rest of the artwork: the playfield, the plastic cut-outs on the field, and even the outside of the cabinet.

About a dozen prototypes are then sent to several test sites to gauge players' reactions. The manufacturer decides on the length of the production run, based on the earning these games achieved during their field trials. This test period also lets the manufacturer identify any technical snags that may have been missed along the way, and correct the problems before the game goes into production.

At last, the new machine is given final approval and full production begins. The manufacturer sells the games to distributors around the world, who in turn resell them to operators who put the machines in arcades, bars and other locations.

SERVING UP THE FINEST EARNINGS!

**It's fresh!
It's fast!
It's hot!**

And it's serving up a full plate of profits and play appeal! DINER has the innovative features, clever theme and total reliability that only Williams can deliver! Most important, DINER is classic Williams pinball that not only gives you a fantastic return on investment, but also retains the highest resale in the business.

ABOVE *Williams'* Diner *(1990) featured backglass animation multiball play and a playfield 'cup shot' that could score more than 3 million points!*

plastic skull to dancing 'Boogie Men'.

Williams' *Diner* (1990) has the look and feel of a 1950s eatery. *Diner* plays a catchy fifties doo-wop tune during multiball and even has impatient 'customers' reminding you that 'you're too slow' if you take too long between shots.

Several major shakeups have occurred in the pinball industry in the last few years. D. Gottlieb and Co., long a family-run operation, was sold to Columbia Pictures in the late seventies; today, it's been renamed Premier Technology and is an independent company managed by industry veteran Gilbert Pollock. And long-standing competitors Williams Electronics and Bally Manufacturing are now under the same roof. Williams bought Bally in late 1988, and although Bally still maintains its own production staff, its machines are assembled only a few feet away from Williams' games.

Collecting pinball machines has become popular recently, as hobbyists restore games that have been gathering dust for years. Several collectors in Phoenix, Arizona, sponsor an annual pinball convention every summer, where flipper enthusiasts from all over the US meet to buy, sell and trade machines. These 'swap-meets' are an ideal place to locate hard-to-find replacement parts, technical information and even original pinball sales brochures.

While video games are still the most popular form of coin-op entertainment, pinball machines are holding their own. Nearly every arcade today has at least two or three pinballs, including some which had only videos until a couple of years ago.

Pinball machines are fun to play because each game is different. The random bumper action means that no two games will ever be exactly alike. You can never truly master a pinball machine because luck plays such an important part in the outcome of the game. Pinball has gone through a more dramatic evolution than any other coin-op game because it's been around longer than most other arcade machines. Even accounting for the ups and downs in popularity, it's likely that we'll be flipping the silver ball around for years to come.

ABOVE *Premier Technology's machines include several innovations, such as photographic backglasses and alphanumeric scoring displays. Spring Break (1987) automatically launches up to four balls at once.*

Today's pinballs are still capturing players with new features. One of the most popular games is Bally's *Elvira and the Party Monsters* (1989) which pictures the 'Mistress of the Dark' on the backglass and has a host of devices on the playfield, from a

*I*n Britain they're called 'fruits'. In Australia they're known as 'poker machines'. And in the United States they're still referred to by their low-down name of ages past. They're simply called slot machines. It wasn't always thus, for the automatic pay-out slot has enjoyed names both grand and grubby over the years, depending on how people and the law looked at them.

In the beginning, like the other coin-ops, they were basically amusement machines. The difference was really one of location – nobody built arcades with slots in them. That would have been too crass. And as the laws were structured, it probably would have been illegal. For while it is true that automatic pay-outs were sometimes legal – somewhere – most times they were illegal almost everywhere. So the games were placed in saloons or, as they became more sophisticated, in the dedicated gambling equivalent of the arcade, the casino.

The pay-outs had their start in the late 1880s and really got rolling in the 1890s. The first pay-out that

can be identified is a machine called the *Eureka Box*, made by the Eureka Box Company in Baltimore, Maryland, in 1888. A small window on the front of the wooden cabinet held coins in a jackpot, and at a certain time, when the weight of the played coins finally tipped the balance scale inside, the pot would dump. Players couldn't wait. So they picked up the box, slapped it and slammed it on the bar, and the coins came out. Needless to say, the *Eureka Box* didn't last long.

When the pay-outs came back in the early 1890s they had slam bars across the top to prevent poking, spiked 'bulldog collars' around their boxy cabinets and, to discourage shaking, were often bolted to the bar or counter. They came in a variety of formats, from simple 3-for-1 machines that returned three coins for the one you played (giving you a net gain of only two) every once in a while, to *Two-Door Bank* and *Pyramid Banker* models that built up large pots like the old *Eurekas*. The John Lighton Machine Company in Syracuse, New York, is credited with

RIGHT The broad-spectrum drugstore of the late 19th century was a maze of clutter and penny-grabbing devices. A Waddell Wooden Ware Works Discount Bicycle Wheel sits on the counter at far right, waiting for a chance taker.

starting the 3-for-1 trend in 1892, with half a dozen more on the market by the next year. One of the more complicated versions was made by the Davis Novelty Company in Elmira, New York, in late 1892 and was produced for another four or five years.

These very early wooden box pay-outs are coveted by collectors as they take you back to the very beginnings of coin-operated amusements. And they are rare. For instance, no example of the *Eureka Box* has ever been found, although at least one example of most others has survived the years.

The American 3-for-1s and the bank machines do not seem to have taken hold in Great Britain or in Europe. Very early in the game the pay-out amusement of choice in France, Germany and the British Isles was the wall machine, capable of being hung on the wall of a pub or *Stube*, out of the way of the serious drinking fraternity. So if you wanted to wager a coin or two against winning back more, you could do so without interfering with the patrons who were there for other amusements.

The ultimate development of these wooden box beauties was the *Three Jackpot* made by the Clawson Slot Machine Company of Newark, New Jersey, between 1893 and the early 1900s. A coin is inserted in the chute at the top of the game, a simple cast-iron mechanism, which then trickles down over pins on a vertical playfield. If it goes into a proper hole, the pot full of money below that hole dumps when you turn a crank or push the coin chute slide once again. Dozens of similar machines were produced by as many new manufacturers in a variety of names, including *Bonanza, Automatic Slot Machine, Investor, Little Casino* and others; yet to this day the Clawson model survives in greater numbers than any other.

This acceptance of the game paved the way for a major sophistication of design, the automatic colour wheel. First created as the *Automatic Check Machine* and *Horseshoes* by Gustav F. W. Schultze in San Francisco in 1893, the idea of a spinning colour wheel that stopped and maybe made pay-outs from an inventory of coins in a long meandering runway inside the machine, and maybe not, was soon being widely

imitated in Brooklyn, New York City, Cincinnati, Detroit and Chicago. Half a dozen, then a dozen, makers turned out large floor machines, with the Mills Novelty Company of Chicago, formed in 1898, becoming the world leader. By the end of the century,

ABOVE *The elegant Mills Novelty Company* Judge *(1899) is typical of the automatic colour-wheel floor machines produced before World War I.* Judge *has a five-way coin head.*

Europe and the UK were importing most of their pay-out machines from Chicago, a pattern that has only recently been altered.

Mills floor model multiple-play colour wheels started with the *Owl*, advanced to the *Judge, Dewey, Chicago, Duplex* and a host of others in both plain and musical models (which gave you *something* for your money even if you lost), including the complicated *Roulette*. The competition grew by leaps and bounds. Caille-Schiemer in Detroit made the *Puck* and, once re-formed as the Caille Brothers Company, virtually matched Mills model for model with 5-way, 6-way, 7-way and larger multiple-play machines (depending where you played your coin, you were picking a colour to win on the wheel – more coins,

more colours) with names like *Eclipse, Centaur, Lion, Black Cat,* their own *Roulette,* later improved and renamed *Peerless,* and a line-for-line matching array of other machines. Other makers, such as the Watling Manufacturing Company (makers of the *Buffalo, Improved Dewey, Original Judge* – which it wasn't – *Cupid, Crown Prince* and others), and the Automatic Tool & Machine Company (makers of the *Star, World* and *Fox*), both in Chicago, did the same thing.

Another Chicago maker was a firm named Paupa & Hochriem, with Joe Paupa the machine-designing brain and Gus Hochriem (who learned his craft from Gustav F. W. Schultze in San Francisco) the sales engineer. Creating a whole new format for pay-out games suited to smaller locations, they developed a series of countertop one-reel machines that made their pay-outs from a stack of trade tokens over a slide that sliced off the proper denomination token once a winner had been hit. The first model was the *Elk* of 1904, followed by the *Pilot* in 1906. This time everyone copied P&H, with *Elk, Pilot, Eagle, Special, Tiger, Baseball* and other models being produced by Mills, Watling, Caille Bros., an outfit called Silver King in Indianapolis, Cowper Manufacturing in Chicago, and other makers. Mills Novelty even appropriated the idea to create their own original one-reeler called *Check Boy* which they marketed as a 'Miniature Dewey'. The die had been cast, and the smaller machines were in. Today they are among the most valuable collectibles of all because of their intricate and often artistic cast-iron cabinets.

Other coin-op chance game formats that were prevalent throughout this pioneering period were the non-pay-outs known as trade stimulators, among the most entertaining coin machines ever made. The idea was not to make actual cash pay-outs but stimulate sales, or trade, at the establishment running the game. It worked like this: take a nickel, play it in a trade stimulator. If the wheel says '2' you get a dime's worth of trade. If it says '1' you still get your nickel's worth, and if it says '3' or '4' or more you get the multiples. A 'No Blanks' machine meant you would never get less than your nickel's worth, which means you always had the chance of getting more for your money. If two similar stores were close to each other, and only one had trade stimulators on the counter, who do you think would get most of the business?

A vast multitude of trade stimulator game formats were made between the late 1880s and the early 1920s that were either sold cheap or were given to stores with large orders for food or confectionery goods. Wrigley's passed out a game called *The Bicycle* when you ordered two crates of stick gum, enough to last a decade in a slow spot. As a result, *The Bicycle* was spinning its numbered wheels on counters all over the United States and Canada. For some reason the idea never caught on elsewhere, but in the

Americas it was endemic. Major 19th- and early 20th-century makers were the Waddell Wooden Ware Works (makers of *The Bicycle*) in Greenfield, Ohio; the Brunhoff Manufacturing Company and the Chas. T. Maley Novelty Company in Cincinnati; the Leo Canda Company, also in Cincinnati; the Drobisch Brothers Company in Decatur, Illinois; the Decatur Fairest Wheel Company, makers of one of the most popular trade stimulators of all called *The Fairest Wheel*, also in Illinois; the M.O. Griswold & Company facing the Mississippi River in Rock Island, Illinois; and of course Mills, Caille, Watling and the other major slot machine makers.

At the time that the Paupa & Hochriem *Elk* was making its appearance, the most popular trade stimulator was the card roller, a five-reel machine that simulated a hand at cards. Dozens of makers produced the machines in confusing profusion. There were variations that played pinochle or, in a three-reel version, policy. But the five-card hand remained the most popular. Until the Puritan Machine Company in Detroit came along. Puritan reduced the show to three number reels, and added a coin separator that made the operator–merchant split an automatic affair. Introduced in 1904, by 1906 the *Puritan* machine was being made by Caille, Mills, Watling and others. Two decades later it was still being made, with the O.D. Jennings Company, a competitor to Mills, producing its own version: *Puritan Girl*.

The idea of three reels – not a new one, but an idea whose time had come – swept the country. Its biggest impression was made in San Francisco where Charlie Fey, perhaps the single most creative genius in the early period of slot machines, picked it up for a machine that would become the standard for automatic pay-out slots for at least the next hundred years. Maybe more. Fey (who also learned his coin-machine-making skills at the hands of Gustav F.W. Schultze by producing machines for him under contract) married the three reels to the slide payout mechanism, and in a brilliant display of non-verbal engineering (Fey just picked up his metalworking file and made things) created a proprietary gambling machine for his own operating routes. His reel symbols were card-playing spots and, in a gesture of patriotism, he named his game the *Liberty Bell*. It made a clang that rang round the world. Surviving the San Francisco Earthquake and Fire of April, 1906, with his prototypes, Fey made a deal with the Mills Novelty Company in Chicago to trade his idea for manufactured machines so he could supply his

routes with new equipment at a minimum of expense. Of the dozens probably made by Fey, only three have survived to become possibly the most valuable vintage slot machines in the world.

Mills re-engineered the game (this time with drawings) as its own *Liberty Bell* and got into production by 1909. It was soon the most popular and successful slot machine to date. Quickly it was copied by Caille,

RIGHT *The Caille Brothers' Operator Bell Deluxe (1912) as made in Detroit. All of the recognized features of the modern slot are here: three reels with fruit symbols, side handle and bottom pay-out cup.*

then Watling, and before the first quarter of the century was out, by just about any maker that produced slots. Caille, and then O.D. Jennings (who had a company called the Industry Novelty Company that bought up old *Liberty Bell* machines and revamped them as their own), saw a way to get around the saloon gambling aspects of the machine by calling it a gum vendor, replacing the card symbols on the reels with different pictures of fruit – pineapple, apple, banana, strawberries and others – to suggest the so-called gum flavours. These reel symbols were intended for placement on machines in drug stores, restaurants, in hotel lobbies and other places where the general public congregated. Mills Novelty bought into the idea the next year, and in 1910 copyrighted its own fruit symbols of lemon, cherry, orange and plum, adding a bell as a logo for its gum line, and a bar symbol that named its gum: Bell-Fruit-Gum. Second only to the suit symbols on playing cards, the Mills fruits became the best-known gambling symbols in the world. Mills named their new machine the *Operator Bell*. Soon, to save time, everybody simply called them Bells, using the same symbols because of their universal acceptance.

The optimum coin-operated gaming invention was now at hand. For the next fifty years the machine was modified upwards and downwards and sideways while still retaining its basic format. Carrying out the gum vendor approach to get around the anti-gambling laws, side vending columns were added. Then multiple column fronts. In the early 1920s Jennings converted the front columns to mints, and everybody copied that. The viability of these confection-vending Bell machines was continually tested in court, but they almost always won (although some judges did wonder why there was so much machinery to deliver a roll of mints). Then, in 1927, the Lincoln Novelty Company in Toledo, Ohio, added a window on the front that contained coins. Hit the three bars and it dumped. It was the first popular Bell machine jackpot. (Actually, Watling had made a similar machine six or seven years earlier, but it didn't catch on.) By the time this fabulous new feature had en-

ABOVE *With saloon locations eliminated by Prohibition (1920–1933) trade stimulators crossed over into legitimate businesses. This Mills Novelty card-* dropping Commercial, far right at checkout counter, is on location at the Ballou-Latimer Drug Store in Boise, Idaho.

ABOVE *That's a lot of machinery to sell a roll of mints, but the subterfuge often worked. This Mills Front O.K. (F.O.K.* 'Bullseye'), made in 1930, had its columns full and is equipped with skill stops situated above the reels.

RIGHT The feature that revolutionized the game. This is the Mills Jackpot ('Poinsettia') of 1930. The front casting stimulates play by suggesting the coins go right down that chute to the pay-out cup.

tered the mainstream of production the world was in the throes of the Great Depression, and the idea of getting something for nothing – or at least for a small wager – was infectious. The jackpot revolutionized the game, and the available locations proliferated. Depression-era law enforcement often turned its head while the people played.

1931 was a bellwether year for slots. The major makers brought out new lines, and Mills Novelty introduced its 'Silent' series. The major feature was the addition of an escalator, or coin transport, that showed the coins played through a small window so that slugs could be revealed and the game stopped by the merchant. Other makers followed suit in one way or the other. Pace machines had a circular escalator, and in 1935 the Watling Manufacturing Company added a large circular escalator on their *Rol-a-tor* line. (Later the machine was redubbed *Rol-a-top* when nobody pronounced the earlier name right, putting emphasis on the 'tor' rather than saying 'Rollater', although some sources suggest that Watling was sued by another manufacturer using a similar name.) Jennings added an escalator that was advanced by a bicycle chain, making it the sturdiest in the industry, which employed this system for another 40 years.

LEFT *The classic twin jackpot Watling* Rol-a-top *Bell machine in its 'Bird of Paradise' cabinet. Never among the most significant slots when they were operating, to collectors the* Rol-a-top *is a prized machine.*

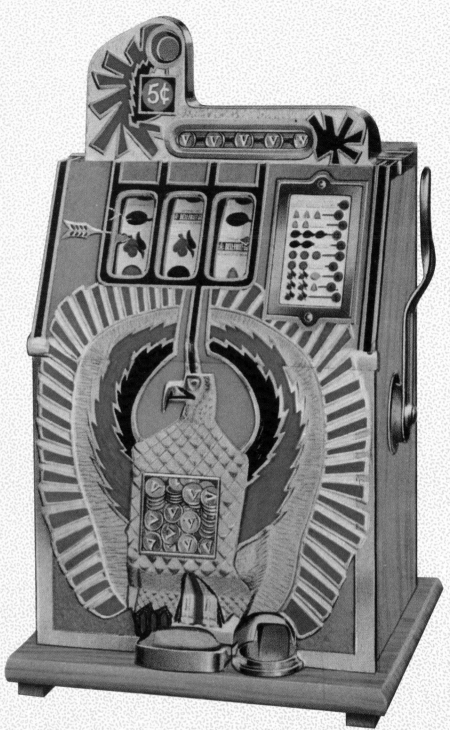

RIGHT *Perhaps the most sought-after Mills escalator collectible. This is the advertising flyer for the Mills 'Silent' War Eagle Bell of 1931. It was also nicknamed the 'Yellow Front'.*

The other major addition in the thirties was design. Deco was rearing its lovely head, as was Moderne and the Machine Age look. Mills Novelty captured the beauty parade with its 'Silent' *War Eagle (1931)*, while Jennings made its mark with the classic Deco styling of its *Little Duke* (1933). Today these machines and their derivatives are collectors' favourites. Even the counter games, the more modern equivalent of the earlier trade stimulators, began to take on the 'Bell' look. Gambling fever had hit the nation coming out of the Depression, and everybody and his brother knew what a slot machine looked like, and had probably played one or more.

All sorts of new machine ideas were tried. The console, a large floor machine usually powered by electricity (something the old machine operators didn't like because they had to learn how to maintain their machines) entered the arena in the middle 1930s. Makers included H. C. Evans, a traditional arcade machine producer; Exhibit Supply, the arcade and pinball maker; and J. H. Keeney, another arcade machine supplier gone console. The new console machines became popular in America, but other countries around the world seem to have been spared their charms. The exception was a game made by the Pace Manufacturing Company called *Paces Races* (1934–45) in which seven small cast-metal horses (or

men in its *Marathon* race model) lurched down a track with one being the pay-out winner. Pay-out coin-op dice games were also popular, as were *Jacks* machines based on the Clawson *Three Jackpot* of forty years earlier. Mills added spice to the play when they introduced their *Mystery* (1933–43) machine, paying odd numbers (three to five coins) rather than evens (standard two to four pay-outs) without announcing the change. Players thought the machine had gone bonkers, and lined up to clean up. But Mills had done it on purpose and it soon flourished.

LEFT *Arguably the most popular slot machine ever made. Mills'* Mystery *introduced the odd three to five coin pay-out schedule. Earlier machines paid two to four. This is the* Blue Front Golden *model of 1937 with gold award tokens.*

Mills also made a game called the *Vest Pocket* that looked like a small portable radio, and tried its hand at other smaller Bells, such as the *Q.T.* Watling made the competitive *Baby Bell*, and Pace the *Bantam*. But for all the variations, from miniaturization to console expansion, it was the classic Bell that remained the players' favourite. By the time World War II had come along (with pay-out slots illegal in Germany and Italy just before the war, an interesting characteristic of totalitarian societies), the classic Bells had taken on a hard and professional look as the artsy-craftsy fronts of the early thirties took a back seat to the militaristic forties. Jennings had its *Standard Chief*, Mills its utilitarian *Chrome* and various spinoffs and Pace its *Comet*; the Watling *Rol-a-top*, meanwhile, remained unchanged.

The one place where slot play became increasingly popular was in Nevada. Coming out of two or more

RIGHT A complete Bell machine is packed into that tiny steel cabinet. The 1940 Mills Vest Pocket has its award schedule on a hinged flap, at right. Flop it over and it covers the reels to make the game look like a radio.

decades of 'blue' laws that made gambling machines illegal as a result of Nevada's rough past, in 1931 the laws were rescinded and gambling under supervision became legal in the state. Expansion was encouraged. It didn't really happen until after World War II when, after four years of pent-up demand, the American people wanted to play. When slot machine production was again authorized (it had been stopped during the war years, as was arcade machine and pinball production) in 1945 the rush was on. Nevada became *the* market, and the post-war production poured in. Mills had redesigned its machines in a modern 'high-top' format, while Jennings went for chrome and lights in its casino *Sun Chief* and, later, four-reel *Buckaroo* models. Another newcomer was the Buckley Manufacturing Company, making an adaptation of the Mills escalator Bells in the form of the *Criss Cross Belle* machines (1948–55).

LEFT *The beginning of the change. This post-World War II machine looks like a pre-war Mills escalator Bell, but is actually a Buckley 1948 Extra Award Criss Cross Belle. The Buckley Bells were among the first post-war Nevada machines.*

All of this happened just in time, for a strong wave of post-war anti-gambling fever was moving across the United States just as the Prohibition against drink did after World War I. It culminated in the Johnson Act signed by President Harold Truman on 2 January 1951, ending the open operation of slot machines in America for decades. Only now are they beginning to creep back for the steamboat gambling on the Mississippi River, and under local mandates. The illegality of the gambling machines didn't stop further development. In fact it increased the activity, only now major efforts were being made to get around the Federal laws. The result was another new machine class called the upright, in which flickering lights make certain scores which are paid off in 'replays', more often than not paid off in cash by the merchant with the replay count tripped back to zero on the machine. Major makers were Auto-Bell, Games Inc. (an outgrowth of the old H. C. Evans firm which went on the auction block), J. H. Keeney, another pinball and arcade machine maker taking the plunge, and Bally, laying back in the weeds waiting to see if the new machines would be acceptable, meantime reaping the benefits of a major export market. Mills Industries solved their problem by re-organizing, and moving to Sparks, later Reno, Nevada as the Bell-O-Matic Company (later Mills Bell-O-Matic). Pace joined Mills out West, as a mass exodus of old slot professionals followed their sun. Jennings stayed in Chicago to ship long distance, also cashing in on the export market by opening up an assembly plant in Bermuda to supply the now burgeoning UK and Commonwealth market without paying the staggering taxes facing a non-British supplier.

The British market really opened up at the 18th Annual British Amusement Trades Exhibition in London in January 1961. The House of Commons had authorized machine play, but only under supervised conditions. That was enough to open the floodgates of machine offerings from around the world, including Japan, where Sega machines, based on (and looking almost exactly like) the Mills *Hightop*, were

vying for business against their American counterparts. What happened changed the industry once again. The American franchise on slot machine production was lost, with Ainsworth and Nutt & Muddle in Australia coming to the fore, as well as other makers in Belgium, Ireland, Denmark, Germany and elsewhere carving out a piece of the pie. A new dynamic had entered the industry, and a raft of new ideas was the harvest to be reaped.

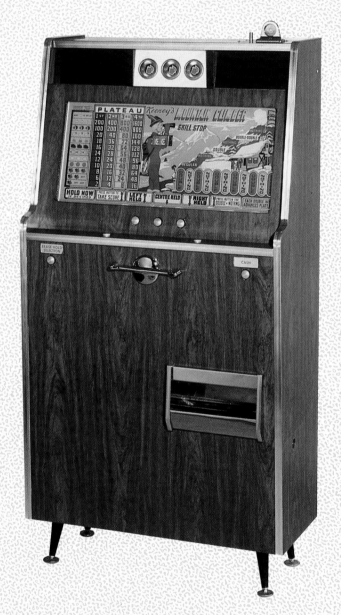

ABOVE *Beating the Johnson Act laws. The Keeney Mountain Climber upright of 1966 has the Panascope symbol display showing three cherries at top centre. As a visualizer it got around the laws governing mechanical 3-reel machines.*

RIGHT *The classic looks of Mills' Hightop, first introduced with the Jewel in 1947. The style endured for over 20 years. It is shown here in the Mills Bell-O-Matic Standard produced in Reno, in around 1960.*

RIGHT *The 'Bally look'. The top glass shows the progressive build-up odds, the wide reels pay on three lines when three coins are entered and the candle at the top lights up and rings when a jackpot hit is made. Bally's* Treasury Special *from the 1970s.*

Just as it looked like the United States had abdicated its stranglehold on slot machine development, the most exciting machine since Charlie Fey's *Liberty Bell* entered the scene. It was created by the Bally Manufacturing Company out of existing components, many of which were *in situ* as a result of Bally's strong position in the export market. The first model was the *Money Honey* (1963), with an incredible pay-out device known as the hopper in its innards. Where the slots of old could pay as much as their stacked coin tubes might hold, they often ran dry for the bigger jackpot pay-outs of Nevada and its casinos. But the hopper, a Nevada innovation based on an adaptation of the coin counter used by banks, increased this capability a hundredfold or more. The modern slot had arrived. Through aggressive merchandising and sales efforts, Bally made its *Money Honey* and subsequent lines the standard of the industry worldwide, bringing with it the 'Bally Look', a flashy and high visibility ID appearance format that allowed any casino to personalize its machines by changing the lighted front panels.

But how different is the modern Bally from the original Fey *Liberty Bell*? In essence, not much. The three reels are still there. And so are the fruit symbols (although a few have been added, like the watermelon), which is what gives the British gambling devices their name of 'fruit' machines. Since the Bally machine revolution a multitude of new manufacturers all over the world have pursued the world gambling machine markets. In large measure they all look alike. A new standard has been set for the playable machines of today and the collectibles of the future. Until something else comes along to create another machine revolution, the look of the slot machine has settled in to an identifiable format that keeps the players coming back for more, and the home enthusiasts licking their chops for the day that they can acquire their own casino machine at a reasonable price and play house.

LEFT *When Seeburg threw its hat into the slot-producing ring, with the games made at Williams Electronics in Chicago in the early 1970s, the appearance retained the 'Bally Look'. This is the 3-Lines Stars and Bars model.*

MATERIALS, TECHNOLOGY AND ART

If an old codger walked out of a Barbary Coast saloon in 1906 right into a modern gambling casino he'd have no problem spotting the fruits. He'd know just how to play, where to put the coin, and how to pull the handle for a reel spin. For over 85 years the integrity of the machine has remained the same. Other coin-op gambling machine formats have come and gone, but the Bell machine has endured, and probably will for many more lifetimes to come. It is the blueprint.

The changes that have occurred, and there are many, have been in the materials, technology and art of the machine. You can date a slot machine by its works and its trimmings. Early machines had clockwork mechanisms released by the dropping of a coin, all encased in often elegant wooden cases and trimmed in brass or nickel plate. Such machines generally date from between 1888 and around 1897, although some exceptions ran into the 20th century.

Large wooden floor machines, with a colour wheel, were made from 1898 through 1917, with the mechanisms made of cast-iron parts, perhaps a bronze part or two, and some cut steel parts. Countertop versions extended into the 1920s and even into the 1930s, but their heyday ended with World War I. Graphics were on the colour wheel, although the front glasswork often carried a silvered machine name surrounded by colourful scrollwork. Floor machines typically weighed from 300 to 650 lb (140 to 300 kg).

Perhaps the most artistic period, and the most sought-after in terms of collectibility, was the brief cast-iron-cabinet phase between the early 1900s and World War I. Highly detailed examples of the foundry patternmaker's art encapsulated the increasingly sophisticated mechanisms of the early 20th century. Both pay-out slots and trade stimulators were enshrined in these marvellous cases, and that included Charlie Fey's original *Liberty Bell*.

Such detailed design ended with World War I as the world slipped into more pragmatic forms of artwork. But there was another problem: the machines were heavy. A Mills Novelty *Operator Bell* of 1910, nicknamed the 'Iron Case', weighed in at around 120 lb (55 kg), no lightweight for its operator to pick up and move around. When wooden cabinets were added in 1915 the weight dropped by 20 lb (9 kg). The real gain came in 1922 when aluminium, brought down in price to working levels after the war, replaced cast iron.

Aluminium also allowed the addition of dramatic cast and painted graphic fronts, with the face of the slot machine becoming an art form.

By 1928 a typical machine weight was 75 lb (35 kg), a workable lift. Side vendor and front vendor features added a little more. By the middle 1930s, with added play features, the weight crept up to 90 pounds and over. It stayed there for three decades, growing a bit as electricity was added as a light-up feature. The advent of the 1963 Bally *Money Honey* and its offspring, made by a growing army of imitators, married the classical three-reel slot machine to electromechanical technology. As more and more features were added, the weight climbed to around 200 lb (90 kg). Weight-saving tricks, such as modern graphics in plastic display panels, formica cabinets and other concessions, were rapidly offset by the newer electronic technologies and the addition of microprocessors. There's no way that a modern slot can be lifted by one person. The machines are right back where they started. But they do look different.

BELOW *The Jennings Improved Little Duke Vender ('Tripl-Duke') of 1933 is a delight of Deco design. The side vendor delivers gum-balls. A lot is packed into this jackpot model.*

CHAPTER 7

Novelty Arcade Games (I)

When you visit most arcades today, you'll probably see video games – lots of them – and maybe a few pinball machines, too. But you might also find several unusual novelty games as well. Some arcades have coin-op basketball shooting games and slot racing machines alongside old favourites like skee ball. Although many novelty games are hot for only a short time, others stay popular for years.

Driving games have always been among players' favourite arcade amusements. Today's driving games all use video screens, but the earlier models produced in the 1940s featured a variety of mechanical designs. *Drive-Mobile*, built in the early forties by the International Mutoscope Company, was a large, upright game with a metal steering wheel on the front of the cabinet; above the wheel, a small toy car was suspended over a rotating 'landscape' drum that pictured roads, scenery and other cars. As the drum turned, you moved the wheel to control the toy car, keeping on the ever-changing road while avoiding collisions with other vehicles. A few years later, Mutoscope produced *New Drive-Mobile*, similar to the original *Drive-Mobile* but in a sit-down cabinet. *New Drive-Mobile* rated your driving skills from 'creeper' to 'road hog' to 'wizard'. *Drive-Mobile* was so popular that Mutoscope produced a two-player model called *Cross Country Race*.

In the fifties, Capital Projector unveiled *Auto Test*, a revolutionary new type of driving game. *Auto Test* replaced the rotating drum with a movie projector, so that you could drive down actual streets and highways rather than miniature 3-D roadway simulations. *Auto Test* also came in a sit-down cabinet, to give you the feeling of being inside a real car. And you could even operate gas and brake pedals for added realism. Capital also produced a machine called *Drive-in Movies*, which resembled *Auto Test* except that it showed colour cartoons rather than streets and roadways.

BELOW Turnpike Tournament, an early 1950s driving game, used actual 8 mm movie footage of city streets and highways. These large driving games were big favourites with young children, and were often found in amusement parks.

Drive-Mobile, Auto Test and other driving games of the 1940s and 1950s were vehicle simulators that tested your everyday driving skills on quiet city streets. But in the sixties, driving games took on grand prix racing themes and offered high-speed thrills to challenge your reflexes.

Games like Chicago Coin's Speed King and Allied Leisure's Drag Races offered fast-moving racetrack action. Many featured gearshift levers so you could shift from 'low' to 'high' gear, and elaborate decorative dashboard designs that included speedometers, tachometers and other gauges. These machines even featured authentic speedway sounds like car horns and squealing tires.

In the early seventies, games like Chicago Coin's Speed Shift featured 'amazing sound effects . . . engine roar synchronized to car speed . . . engine blows on excessive RPM . . . tyres squeal when race-car swerves off race-track . . . grinding of gears!' and other innovations, according to the maker. These driving games were especially popular among teenagers, although young children enjoyed them, too.

Chicago Coin's 1975 Speedway is a classic driving game. Speedway was based on a machine called Indy 500, manufactured by Kansai Seiki International of Australia. You controlled a small toy racing car, mounted in front of the picture screen. During the game, you manoeuvred the car on the moving track projected on the screen, while avoiding collisions with the other cars and the guard rails. Each collision took five seconds off the game clock, so the fewer accidents you had, the higher your score would be.

LEFT Chicago Coin was the leading manufacturer of driving games in the sixties and seventies; many of the company's machines – including Speed Shift – featured realistic motor racing sound effects and can still be found in arcades to this day.

Speedway required fast reflexes and split-second strategy decisions, and was much more intense and challenging than the passive driving simulators of the 1940s and 1950s.

Some driving games used miniature scale-model cars and fluorescent lighting to create a 3-D effect. Bally's *Road Runner* and Midway's *Dune Buggy* both used black lights to enhance the colourful playfields which seemed to change in size and layout throughout the game.

Southland Engineering built two coin-operated slot-racing games in the mid sixties. *Speedway* and *Time Trials* each contained a pair of miniature racing cars on a two-level, figure-8 track inside a pinball-style cabinet. You could either race against the clock or against another player, as you tried to complete 20 laps during the one-minute game. Other companies, including American Machine & Foundry, Innovative Concepts in Entertainment and All-Tech also produced coin-op slot racing games.

ABOVE *Chicago Coin's Speedway (1975) was one of the most popular driving games ever built, but by the late seventies, video driving games had replaced traditional electromechanical driving games like Speedway.*

RIGHT *Little Indy was a coin-operated slot-racing game. Ten cents allowed you to steer the car around an oval track for half a minute.*

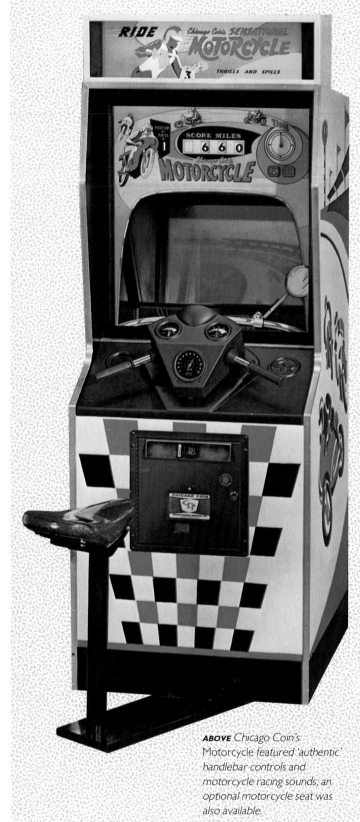

ABOVE Chicago Coin's Motorcycle *featured 'authentic' handlebar controls and motorcycle racing sounds; an optional motorcycle seat was also available.*

Chicago Coin's *Motorcycle* (1974) offered 'all the excitement, sound and spectacular realism of speed demon raceway driving. Player controls an actual scale model motorcycle in raceway competition with other motorcycles!' The game featured realistic handlebar acceleration and even had a bike seat. Like most driving games of the sixties and seventies, *Motorcycle* operated on a timer, letting you score as many points as you could before the clock ran out. Allied Leisure's *Chopper* was also designed for realism; like *Motorcycle*, it featured handlebar controls and a cycle seat. *Chopper* let you control a small animated cyclist that would tilt from side to side as you moved the handlebars.

Genco's *Motorama* (1957) let you manoeuvre a miniature car inside a glass-enclosed cabinet. Points were scored for steering through narrow lanes and across steep ramps. Genco's 1957 *Space Age* was nearly identical to *Motorama*, except that you controlled an army truck removing radioactive waste from a missile testing base!

Genco's *Jet Pilot* gave you control of a small, replica Air Force plane that flew through the air. Actually, the aircraft was connected to a post in the centre of the glass-enclosed cabinet and simply circled around 12 times during the minute-long game. Twelve perfect landings scored a replay and earned you the title of 'jet pilot'. When *Jet Pilot* was released in 1957, it was a hit with players who loved the action and animation of the game, but it wasn't until about a decade later that the concept was revived.

Animated helicopter games were among the most popular arcade novelties of the late sixties. Instead of a jet, you steered a scale-model helicopter inside a glass-enclosed dome. You could raise or lower the chopper while it circled, control its speed, make it fly backwards and hover. The moulded 3-D playfields had hills and valleys, and the object was to raise and lower the chopper as it circled, and touch the checkpoints scattered throughout the cabinet. The spinning propellers and realistic engine sounds made these games stunning to look at – but not much fun to play, because the action was rather repetitive.

Mechanical 'flying bomber' games were popular during the 1960s and early 1970s, but they couldn't compete with the more realistic action found on video games. Chicago Coin's *Flying Tiger*, *Night Bomber* and *Sky Battle* were just a few of these games, which put you at the controls of a fighter jet; when enemy aircraft were spotted, you could drop bombs and fire machine guns while you piloted your plane. Every manufacturer produced at least one of these flying bomber games, including Williams (*Flotilla*), Allied Leisure (*Sonic Fighter*) and Midway (*The Invaders*). A similar game, Bally's *Subpack*, was set under water 'with rippling bubbles and wave-shadows – so wet and watery looking you think you might get splashed,' according to the company.

ABOVE *'Flying Bomber' games like Chicago Coin's* Night Bomber *were popular for a short time in the early 1970s, but these machines were unable to compete with the more versatile video games that were introduced at approximately the same time.*

RIGHT *Scale-model helicopter flying games like Midway's* Whirly Bird *were popular in the late 1960s. You scored points by manoeuvring the chopper into electronic checkpoints in the interior of the cabinet.*

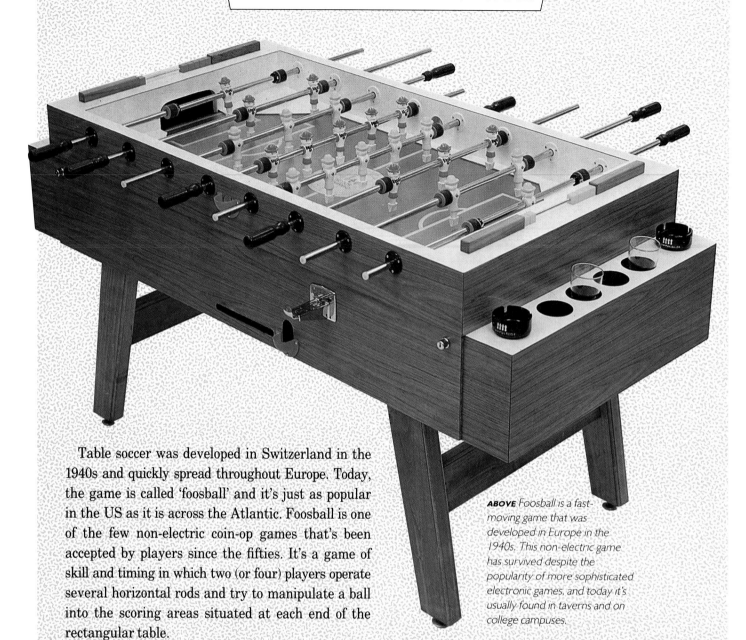

ABOVE *Foosball is a fast-moving game that was developed in Europe in the 1940s. This non-electric game has survived despite the popularity of more sophisticated electronic games, and today it's usually found in taverns and on college campuses.*

Table soccer was developed in Switzerland in the 1940s and quickly spread throughout Europe. Today, the game is called 'foosball' and it's just as popular in the US as it is across the Atlantic. Foosball is one of the few non-electric coin-op games that's been accepted by players since the fifties. It's a game of skill and timing in which two (or four) players operate several horizontal rods and try to manipulate a ball into the scoring areas situated at each end of the rectangular table.

Foosball became popular in the US in the mid 1970s – especially on college campuses where tournaments were regularly held. Today, the game is found primarily in bars and pubs where the competition is as fierce as ever. Foosball is an aggressive game that demands a great deal of physical involvement and appeals mainly to men.

In 1982, Innovative Concepts in Entertainment (ICE) introduced *Chexx*, a hockey-themed version of foosball. The small playing figures appeared to skate on the surface of the playfield, rather than spinning around like foosball figures. *Chexx* had a plastic dome over the playing area with a 'scoreboard' mounted at

the top, and featured realistic crowd noises such as cheers and boos. ICE's soccer-themed follow-up game called *Kixx* wasn't nearly as successful as *Chexx*.

Air hockey is another popular two-player table game. Although not quite as intense as foosball, it's a fast-moving game that's being promoted as a sport through national tournaments sponsored by a manufacturer of the games. The first air hockey games were unveiled in 1973, and were an instant hit. The object is to shoot a flat, plastic puck into the goal at the opposite end of the table. The puck actually floats on a cushion of air that's pumped through thousands of pinhole-sized openings in the tabletop. Hard-hit

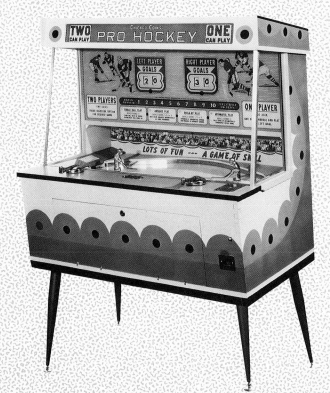

LEFT *Chicago Coin's Pro Hockey (1961) was based on the company's 1949 hit game Goalee; Chicago Coin built a string of popular hockey-themed games in the sixties and early seventies.*

pucks can sometimes go flying through the air or hit an unwary player's fingers, so many arcades have posted signs reading 'Not Responsible for Injuries – Play at your Own Risk' above the tables. Like foosball, many air hockey players are very loyal to the game, practising several times a week.

Brunswick's *Air Handball* and US Billiards' *Air Jai-Ali* were both produced in the mid seventies and were more compact than other air hockey tables because the players stood side-by-side and rebounded the puck off the back wall of the machine. Traditional two-sided air hockey tables have always been players' favourites, though.

A lot of coin-op hockey-themed games have been produced, but few have been as popular as Chicago Coin's *Goalee*. *Goalee* (1949) was very simple to play and understand; you operated a control handle which directed an animated goalkeeper to spin either clockwise or anti-clockwise, and tried to knock the balls into the scoring pocket at the opposite end of the playfield. With its wooden art-deco cabinet and unique artwork, *Goalee* remained popular for years. Chicago Coin even released a similar game in 1961 called *Pro Hockey*, with an updated cabinet and artwork. Chicago Coin also produced a smaller version of

Goalee, in a pinball-style cabinet, called *Criss Cross Hockey* (1958), which featured a unique bonus system *à la* noughts and crosses (tic-tac-toe). Other Chicago Coin hockey games, such as *Hockey Champ* and *Slap Shot Hockey* (both produced in the early seventies) weren't nearly as popular.

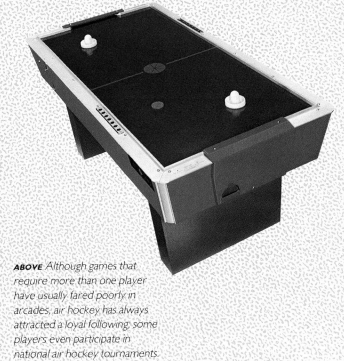

ABOVE *Although games that require more than one player have usually fared poorly in arcades, air hockey has always attracted a loyal following; some players even participate in national air hockey tournaments.*

RIGHT *One of the most popular arcade games ever created was Chicago Coin's Basketball Champ, which featured two small metal figures with moveable arms. The object was to toss the walnut-sized basketballs through the hoop at the back of the cabinet.*

LEFT *The smiling, round-faced characters on* Basketball Champ *appeared on several of Chicago Coin's games in the forties and early fifties.*

Other sports were also adapted as coin-op amusement games. Genco's *Basketball* was a one- or two-player machine that boasted 'all the speed and excitement of a real basketball game . . . the fascination of "sinking" a long shot . . . the thrill of a lucky rebound'. *Basketball* contained two ten-inch metal manikins inside a glass booth. The manikins were designed to hold a walnut-sized ball at waist level and toss it into the air towards the baskets suspended inside the cabinet. Squeezing the handgrip control caused the manikin to shoot at the baskets, but you had to make your shots quickly because one of the 12 balls would be released every five seconds. If two people played *Basketball*, each would aim for his own baskets, but if your manikin threw the ball into one of your opponent's baskets, he would receive the points. To make the game even more interesting, the baskets would register different scores at various times throughout the game. *Basketball* was one of the most popular machines ever built by Genco; a similar game called *Pro Basketball* (1961) by Chicago Coin proved almost as popular. Exidy's 1975 *Old Time Basketball* reintroduced this classic arcade game to a new generation of players.

Only a few novelty arcade games have been based on American football, but one of the most interesting was Williams' *Touchdown*, produced in the late 1950s. *Touchdown*'s playfield was designed like a baseball-themed pitch and bat game, but featured football scoring and artwork; it even included the same back-box animation as that found on Williams' baseball machines. Although *Touchdown* wasn't particularly popular, Williams released two more pitch and bat football games, both called *Gridiron*, in 1969 and 1984. Novelty games can't capture the rough-and-tumble action of real football, although some video games have come close to duplicating the feel of the sport.

Not all baseball machines used a pitch and bat format. *Magic Baseball* by the Shelden, Dickson & Steven Mfg. Co. offered a completely different approach. This 1966 machine contained a plastic baseball suspended on a jet of compressed air that 'floated' beside a mechanical ballplayer. You adjusted the air pressure to raise or lower the ball, and when you were satisfied with its position, you swung the bat. If you had lined up the ball correctly, you'd hit a home run – otherwise, you'd register a strike. *Magic Baseball* used black lighting for a 3-D effect and gave you nine swings per game. This concept proved to be a one-off, however, failing to catch on with many players.

Chicago Coin's *Mini Baseball* was a compact, wall-mounted game designed for locations with limited space. You simply shot a small, plastic ball through rolldown lanes marked 'single', 'double', 'triple', 'home run' and 'out' on a vertical playfield. Scoring was the same as in real baseball, with three outs ending the game. *Mini Baseball* also included solid state sounds like crowd cheers and 'raspberries'. Despite its simplistic design and small size, *Mini Baseball* was quite popular.

Bally's *Big Bat* (1984) was a miniature batting cage, and had a trigger-grip control handle that swung a bat inside the glass-enclosed cabinet. When the plastic ball was shot toward the paddle, you timed your swing to send the ball flying into the bleachers. *Big Bat* played tunes like 'Take Me out to the Ball Game' and even included a vendor's voice shouting 'peanuts and popcorn!' Unfortunately, many of these machines couldn't withstand the constant pounding of the ball and it's not unusual to find *Big Bat* games that have been taped up to conceal the damage.

In the mid 1960s, several golf games appeared which are just as popular among collectors today as they were with players when they were built.

ABOVE, LEFT Coin-operated dartboards featuring digital scoring and electronic sounds have proven popular in pubs and taverns throughout Europe and the United States. These games use specially designed soft-tip darts rather than conventional darts.

ABOVE, RIGHT Chicago Coin's Mini-Baseball was a small, vertical game designed for places where full-sized machines couldn't fit. The game could either be mounted on the wall or, alternatively, placed on a wooden pedestal base.

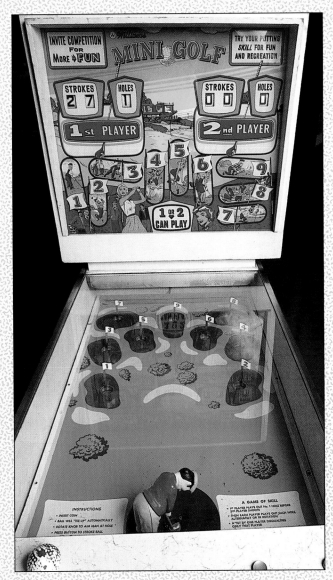

appeared – for the first time in 25 years – on a game called *Little Pro* by Bromley. Their *Little Pro* is set on a reproduction of a miniature golf course, complete with rotating windmills and other tricky mini golf hazards.

Several full-sized coin-op putting greens, designed for arcades, have been produced, including *Pro-Golfer*, built by Forward Industries in the fifties. The machine had three holes which opened one at a time during the game. You received nine balls for a dime, and up to four people could play together.

Darts is another recreational pastime that's become a popular coin-op novelty. The game of darts has long been enjoyed in bars, and several companies are producing coin-op dartboards that include space-age electronic sounds and small video screens that display the scores! You can pick one of several scoring variations (some machines offer up to eight different choices) – and, of course, these games automatically tally the scoring. Because these dartboards have hundreds of tiny scoring holes and the darts have plastic tips, many purists won't play coin-op dart games. Still, these dartboards have become very popular in many bars where weekly tournaments are held. One of the leading manufacturers of coin-op dart games, Arachnid, sells clothes, bumper stickers, patches and even trophies to stimulate interest in tournaments. According to Arachnid's promotional material, 'English Mark Darts is not only entertainment but a sport . . . a skill that can be nurtured and polished but never perfected'.

Bumper pool was one of the hottest games of the late 1950s, and just about every tournament game company produced a few of these machines. Many of these coin-op bumper pool tables were one- or two-sided, taking up less space than conventional four-sided pool tables. Some clever bumper pool variations were produced, including Chicago Coin's *Croquet* (1958), which had semi-circular hoops, like an outdoor croquet field, on the playing surface.

Williams described its *Mini Golf* as 'the first realistic 9-hole putting green under glass' – and that's exactly what it was. You controlled a small metal golfer on a rotating base and aimed for the lit hole on the pinball-sized golf course; because the holes were scattered around the playfield, you could select either a hard or an easy stroke. The game lasted until you got through all nine holes or took 27 strokes. Southland's *Little Pro* was almost identical to *Mini Golf* – it even included the same animated golfer! Chicago Coin's *Par Golf* and Williams' *Hollywood Driving Range* each featured a row of targets at the top of the playfield, instead of a miniature putting green. Interestingly, the same animated metal golfer has just re-

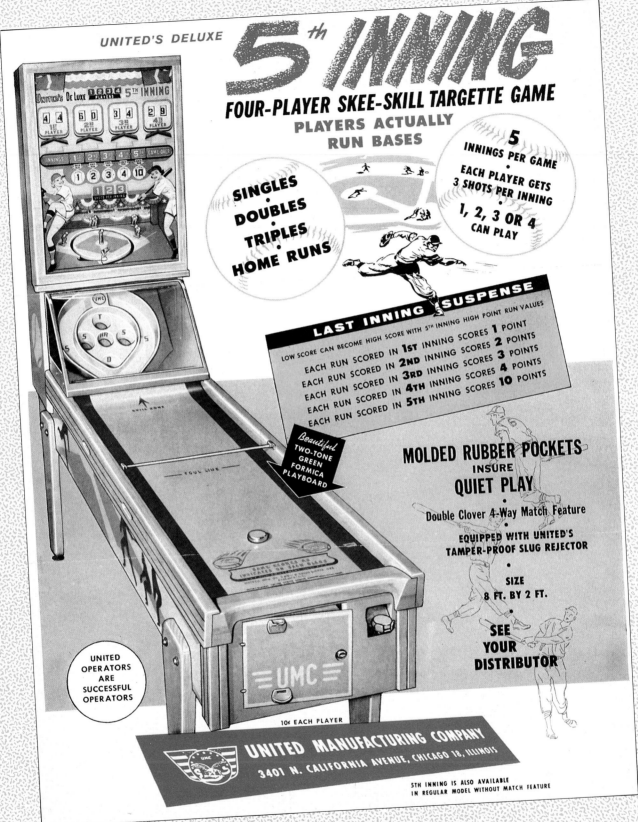

UNITED'S DELUXE

5th INNING

FOUR-PLAYER SKEE-SKILL TARGETTE GAME

PLAYERS ACTUALLY RUN BASES

SINGLES · DOUBLES · TRIPLES · HOME RUNS

5 INNINGS PER GAME · EACH PLAYER GETS 3 SHOTS PER INNING · **1, 2, 3 OR 4** CAN PLAY

LAST INNING SUSPENSE

LOW SCORE CAN BECOME HIGH SCORE WITH 5TH INNING HIGH POINT RUN VALUES

EACH RUN SCORED IN **1ST** INNING SCORES **1** POINT
EACH RUN SCORED IN **2ND** INNING SCORES **2** POINTS
EACH RUN SCORED IN **3RD** INNING SCORES **3** POINTS
EACH RUN SCORED IN **4TH** INNING SCORES **4** POINTS
EACH RUN SCORED IN **5TH** INNING SCORES **10** POINTS

Beautiful TWO-TONE GREEN FORMICA PLAYBOARD

MOLDED RUBBER POCKETS INSURE QUIET PLAY

Double Clover 4-Way Match Feature

EQUIPPED WITH UNITED'S TAMPER-PROOF SLUG REJECTOR

SIZE 8 FT. BY 2 FT.

SEE YOUR DISTRIBUTOR

UNITED OPERATORS ARE SUCCESSFUL OPERATORS

10¢ EACH PLAYER

UNITED MANUFACTURING COMPANY

3401 N. CALIFORNIA AVENUE, CHICAGO 18, ILLINOIS

5TH INNING IS ALSO AVAILABLE IN REGULAR MODEL WITHOUT MATCH FEATURE

ABOVE *Shuffle targette games like United's Deluxe 5th Inning were a cross between puck bowling machines and skee ball games. The technique was to slide a round metal puck down a wooden alley towards a series of scoring pockets.*

When shuffle bowling machines became popular in the 1950s, manufacturers began designing some non-bowling shuffle games. Shuffle 'targettes' were about the same size and shape as puck bowling games, but instead of bowling pins, these machines had several scoring cups like those found on skee ball games. United's *Deluxe Shuffle Targette* (1954) was the first game of this type – and it was a hit with players. United produced a series of these shuffle targettes throughout the 1950s and 1960s, including *Comet, Venus, Playboy, Rumpus* and *Kickapoo*. Probably the most interesting shuffle targette game was United's *5th Inning* (1955). This baseball-themed machine included an animated base-running unit in the backbox, and scored like real baseball with 'singles', 'doubles', 'triples' and 'home runs'. Shuffle targettes were reintroduced in the 1980s, with Williams' *Kickapoo II* and Meltec's *Target Ace*, although neither game met with success.

Other shuffle games featured bouncing balls rather than bowling pins. United's *Jupiter* and *Shooting Star* each had 25-hole grids containing several rubber balls; you aimed the puck to launch some or all of the balls, using the same strategy found on Williams' late fifties rifle games. Points (and replays) were scored for three, four or five balls in a row. Chicago Coin produced two bouncing balls shuffle games of its own – *Rocket Shuffle* and *Shuffle Explorer*. For a short time, these games were very popular; in fact, according to a 1958 Chicago Coin press release, '*Rocket Shuffle* reports reaching us have been fantastic. Even now, after months of on-location operation, this game continues to maintain unbelievably high profits. For this reason, we definitely believe that this type of game is here to stay for some time to come.' But as the novelty of these games wore off, Chicago Coin and United returned to building more traditional shuffle bowling games. Chicago Coin revived the concept one last time in 1973 on *Las Vegas Shuffle*, but the results were disappointing.

LEFT *A puck was used to launch the bouncing rubber balls that were reflected in the backglass of Chicago Coin's* Shuffle Explorer *– but the novelty never appeared to attract a great deal of players.*

Chicago Coin introduced a few more unusual shuffle games in the 1960s and early 1970s, including *Top Brass, World Series* and *Bull's-Eye Drop Ball*. Chicago Coin's *All American Basketball* (1972) even featured backbox animation, with two figures that shot for the baskets if you aimed the puck correctly.

United's *Pool Alley* (1956) resembled a shuffle bowler – but with one big difference: instead of a puck, you shot a pool ball at the pins! The rules were the same as in bowling; you had two shots to hit all ten pins in each of the ten frames. This attempt at combining two popular games fell far short of United's expectations, though.

At about the same time as United introduced *Pool Alley*, Genco unveiled *Shuffle Pool*, a billiards game in a shuffle alley cabinet. The 15 pool balls at the end of the alley were actually hollow, plastic balls that were suspended over the playfield; small lights inside the balls would go out when they were 'hit' by the cue ball. You had 18 shots to sink as many balls as you could. Because the 15 balls in *Shuffle Pool* remained in the same position rather than scattering in all directions like real billiard balls, the game resembled bowling more than pool. Genco called *Shuffle Pool* 'America's newest all-location amusement rage', but the game never lived up to the hype.

RIGHT *United's Bank Pool combined two of the most popular pastimes of the late 1950s – billiards and bowling – as you tried to hit the pins with a cue ball. The game received only a lukewarm response from most players.*

In 1989, Classic Creations introduced *Hop Shot*, a combination of pool and skee ball. Using a cue stick, you shot a pool ball into the circular scoring pockets at the end of the cabinet. *Hop Shot* was designed for bars, but the game was also available with an optional ticket dispenser for redemption arcades.

Although skee ball had been around since the 1930s, a new generation of players discovered the game in the mid 1950s. Suddenly, every game company had a skee ball machine in production, and each added some new wrinkle to the game. Chicago Coin's *Ski-Bowl* awarded bonus balls and frames, Genco's *Skill Ball* offered double and triple scoring in selected frames, and Exhibit's *Ringer Ball* gave you a choice of tossing or rolling the balls. Keeney's *Bowlette*, Williams' *Roll-a-Ball* and Bally's *Bank Ball* were just some of the other skee ball games that were produced. This boom was only short-lived, but skee ball remained popular during the sixties.

In 1967, automatic ticket dispensers started appearing on skee ball machines, and the games' popularity increased again. Along with the traditional skee ball machines produced by the Philadelphia Toboggan Company/Skee Ball, companies like Chicago Coin and Midway introduced skee ball games of their own. In 1974, the first electronic skee ball alleys appeared, and the game entered the computer age.

Skee Ball estimated that by the mid 1980s, over 20,000 skee ball alleys were in operation across the US.

RIGHT Chicago Coin's Roto Ball tried to cash in on the skee ball craze of the late fifties. Nearly every game manufacturer had a skee ball lane on the market.

RIGHT In the late 1960s, quiz games were found in drug stores, restaurants and other places where you wouldn't expect to find coin-op games. These machines were popular among adults who had never played coin-op amusement games before.

LEFT *A wireless remote control box was used to play wall games like Midway's* Table Tennis *from the comfort of your barstool. Although these games were briefly popular in the mid 1970s, they quickly disappeared when games like* Space Invaders *and* Asteroids *appeared.*

Quiz games were popular in the sixties and early seventies, and are still on the up and up in the UK. Nutting Industries, the leading manufacturer of these machines, called them 'educational as well as entertaining'. After you selected a category from such choices as 'movies and television', 'sports and games', 'people and places' and 'general knowledge', you would answer five or six multiple choice questions. Points were awarded for speed and accuracy, so you had to think fast; the quicker you answered, the higher your score would be. Nutting also produced several 'specialty' quiz games, including *Sports World* and *Golf IQ*. Most quiz games contained anywhere from 1,600 to 2,800 different multiple choice questions displayed in a random sequence, so no two games were ever exactly alike. Nutting also produced two-player quiz games which let you compete against someone else while racing the game clock.

Allied Leisure introduced a different kind of quiz game called *Unscramble* in the early 1970s. A scrambled three-letter word appeared on the screen, and you tried to unscramble it as quickly as possible. If that sounds too easy, it was. Allied discovered that players liked the concept of *Unscramble*, but learned that three-letter words were too simple for most people, so the company developed *Unscramble Deluxe*, which used four- and five-letter words.

Allied also produced the unusual *What Zit?* (1973) which challenged you to identify objects from fractional segments projected on the screen. After you saw the first small segment, additional segments were added every four seconds until the object was complete, but the more you saw before you could correctly identify the object, the less you would score.

In the early seventies, several companies produced games designed to fill unused space on bar walls. These large 'wall games' were about 32 inches high and 53 inches wide – but only about 8 inches deep, so they looked like giant picture screens. You could play these games while you sat at the bar by pressing a button on a small, portable remote control box, which let you shift some of the moving lights on the screen. But there were several drawbacks to wall games. For one thing, the coin slot was attached to the wall unit, so you still had to leave your seat at the bar to drop in your quarter. And the game would be useless if there were people standing between you and the wall unit, blocking the infra-red transmission of the remote control box. The superior game action on videos also led to the demise of wall games, which played much like today's toy arcade machines. Although the popularity of wall games was short-lived, research and development on other new types of novelty arcade games continues.

BRITISH-MADE MACHINES

The US has always been the leading producer of coin-op machines; according to some estimates, the country manufactures more than 90 per cent of the world's games. Still, some British companies have produced a number of arcade games, too, including Nixson's of Littlehampton, which built coin-op novelties like *Noughts and Crosses* and *Ski Run* in the 1970s. Nixson's *Power Boat Race* was a driving game set on the water – you used a 'ship's wheel' to steer. And the company's *Action Stations* was a large, torpedo-shooting game with two full-sized swivelling periscopes built into the cabinet.

Helibomber, produced by London Coin Machines in the late 1960s, was similar to the helicopter flying games made by companies like Williams and Midway. Instead of trying to touch checkpoints with your miniature chopper, though, you had to drop a 'bomb' (actually a steel ball) on a target area.

Ash & Allen produced the *Challenger* foosball table in the 1960s. Although the company called itself 'The Football Machine Specialists', it only built these machines for a short time. And Ameco Amusement Equipment, which was founded in 1932, produced skee ball machines until the company went out of business in the 1970s.

One of the most successful British game manufacturers was Alca Electronics, several of whose machines were popular in the US as well as in the UK, including *Flying Circus*. This 1971 game let you manoeuvre a 3-D plane through a series of hoops inside a black-lit cabinet. Alca Electronics' *Target UFO* was a futuristic shooting game that rotated inside a large vertical metal framework; as you moved your gun to fire, the entire machine would swivel on the circular base.

Alfred Crompton produced a few novelty arcade games in the 1970s, including an animated boxing game called *Knockout*, although the company is better known for its 'penny pusher' machines. Several other British companies, including Streets Automatic Machine and Harry Levy Amusements, specialize in these pusher games, which are still enjoyed in many seaside arcades in the UK today.

BELOW *British-based Alca's* Flying Circus *was one of the most popular games produced in England. Black lighting inside the cabinet gave the machine an unusual 3-dimensional effect.*

CHAPTER 8
Novelty Arcade Games (2)

Some novelty arcade games defy classification. They're so different from other amusement games that they're in a class by themselves. MCI's *Airball*, for instance, was one of the most unusual games ever produced. You manoeuvred a table tennis ball, supported on a column of air, through several targets suspended inside the cabinet. The fluorescent black lighting used in this 1972 machine created an eerie, magical effect; whistles, chimes and warbles were among the audio effects.

The Safe, also produced by MCI, tested your safe-cracking skills. You tried to open a mechanical strong-box in less than a minute using the electronic clues provided. If you worked out the correct code from among the four billion possible combinations, the safe door would swing open and a siren would sound.

RIGHT *Amateur safecrackers could use the electronic clues on MCI's* The Safe *to help open the vault. The machine selected a different combination for every single game.*

Taito's *Ice Cold Beer* was billed as 'a unique adult game targeted for taverns, built for bars!' *Ice Cold Beer* (1983) had a hole-studded vertical playfield and a horizontal player-controlled bar that moved up and down over the field. At the start of the game, the bar would drop to the bottom of the field, and a steel ball would be automatically loaded onto it. You used two joystick controls to raise or lower each end of the bar independently as you tried to direct the ball into the randomly lit hole, while avoiding the other 'trap holes' on the playfield. *Ice Cold Beer* really tested your co-ordination, and was also offered as *Zeke's Peak* for arcades.

Fire Escape (1984) was another game which required patience and co-ordination as you manipulated a steel ball down a vertical 'fire escape'. The game, produced by Innovative Concepts in Entertainment (ICE), featured water valve controls and fire engine sounds.

When man first landed on the moon in 1969, space-themed arcade games were common. Bally's *Space Flight* let you land a scale model of a lunar module on an orbiting, black-lit moon. You were guided by actual mission control reports during the game, because *Space Flight* included an eight-track tape with authentic recordings of astronauts' voices. Cointronics' *Lunar Lander* was almost identical to *Space Flight*, even down to the astronauts' voices saying 'Tranquility Base here, the Eagle has landed' at the end of the game. *Lunar Lander* rated your skill on a sliding scale: 'Astronaut', 'Expert', 'A-OK', 'Novice' or 'Earthbound'.

Chicago Coin's *Apollo-14* (1970) let you complete an outer-space docking, as you guided a small spacecraft alongside a large command ship. *Apollo-14* featured spectacular special effects; for instance, if your spacecraft crashed into the command ship, both vessels would disintegrate with a loud explosion and a flash of burning rocket fuel! *Apollo-14* had an unusual cabinet with a large 'viewing bubble' and a detailed reproduction of a spacecraft control panel.

In the late 1960s, Allied Leisure Industries unveiled an unusual arcade game called *Monkey Bizz*.

You controlled a metal hook suspended inside the cabinet, and tried to snare the plastic monkeys lying on the bottom. *Monkey Bizz* was the first game produced by Allied, a company formerly known as All-Tech Industries, which had specialized in kiddie rides and grip testers. *Monkey Bizz* was plagued by mechanical design problems, though, and very few of them were built.

Monkey Bizz wasn't the first monkey-themed amusement game. In the forties, Industrial Engineering produced *Monkey Climb*, a large animated game which contained several furry palm-tree-climbing monkeys. You pulled a plunger and launched a small ball into a circular playfield to determine how many steps the monkey would ascend at a time. You could either race against another player (who shot his own ball into a separate playfield) or against the machine-controlled 'pace monkey' if you were playing alone. The 15-inch plush monkeys (nicknamed Wilbur, Gramps, Jazoo and Speed) wore colourful clothing and turned their heads from side to side as they moved, so that *Monkey Climb* was a sure-fire attention getter.

ABOVE *Innovative Concepts in Entertainment's* Fire Escape *(1984) was one of the few mechanical amusement games produced in the 1980s, when video was king. The game's sound effects included fire engine sirens.*

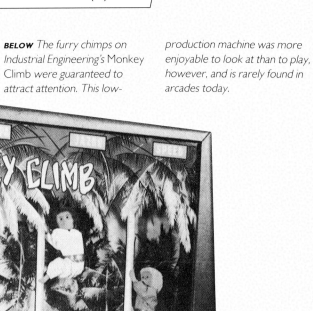

BELOW *The furry chimps on Industrial Engineering's* Monkey Climb *were guaranteed to attract attention. This low-production machine was more enjoyable to look at than to play, however, and is rarely found in arcades today.*

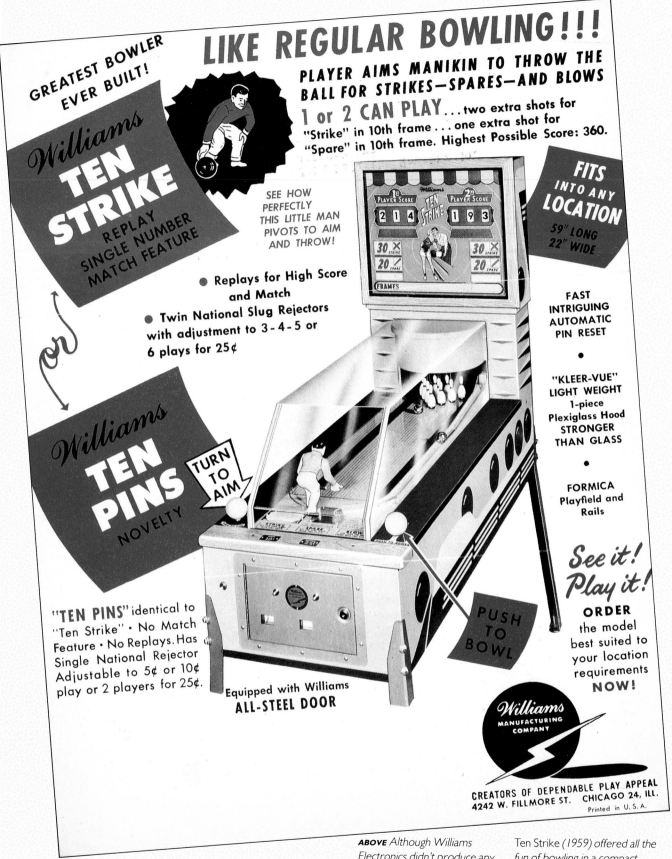

GREATEST BOWLER EVER BUILT!

LIKE REGULAR BOWLING!!!

PLAYER AIMS MANIKIN TO THROW THE BALL FOR STRIKES—SPARES—AND BLOWS

1 or 2 CAN PLAY...two extra shots for "Strike" in 10th frame...one extra shot for "Spare" in 10th frame. Highest Possible Score: 360.

Williams TEN STRIKE

REPLAY
SINGLE NUMBER
MATCH FEATURE

SEE HOW PERFECTLY THIS LITTLE MAN PIVOTS TO AIM AND THROW!

● Replays for High Score and Match
● Twin National Slug Rejectors with adjustment to 3-4-5 or 6 plays for 25¢

or

Williams TEN PINS

NOVELTY

TURN TO AIM

"TEN PINS" identical to "Ten Strike" • No Match Feature • No Replays. Has Single National Rejector Adjustable to 5¢ or 10¢ play or 2 players for 25¢.

Equipped with Williams **ALL-STEEL DOOR**

PUSH TO BOWL

FITS INTO ANY LOCATION

59" LONG
22" WIDE

FAST INTRIGUING AUTOMATIC PIN RESET

●

"KLEER-VUE" LIGHT WEIGHT 1-piece Plexiglass Hood STRONGER THAN GLASS

●

FORMICA Playfield and Rails

See it! Play it!

ORDER the model best suited to your location requirements NOW!

Williams
MANUFACTURING COMPANY

CREATORS OF DEPENDABLE PLAY APPEAL
4242 W. FILLMORE ST.   CHICAGO 24, ILL.
Printed in U. S. A.

ABOVE *Although Williams Electronics didn't produce any conventional bowling machines or shuffle alleys until the mid sixties, the company's popular* Ten Strike *(1959) offered all the fun of bowling in a compact pinball-style cabinet, and featured a small metal manikin that rolled a marble-sized ball.*

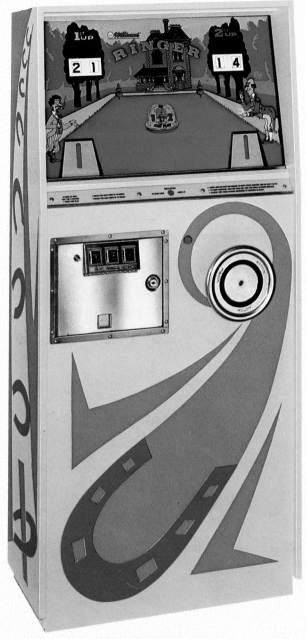

ABOVE Norm Clark designed Williams' Ringer (1973). It was one of the simplest coin-op novelty games ever produced – and one of the most successful in addition.

Williams Electronics has produced some of the most innovative novelty arcade games, along with pinball machines, bowlers, gun games, baseballs and videos. *Sidewalk Engineer* (1956) put you at the controls of a miniature remote-control bulldozer, and let you shift simulated gravel around a glass-enclosed cabinet. *Sidewalk Engineer* was really a coin-op toy rather than a game; there was no scoring on the machine, and you simply manipulated the bulldozer through the gravel for 60 seconds.

Williams' 1958 *Ten Strike* was one of the most popular coin-op novelties of its decade. Similar to the miniature bowling games of the late 1930s, *Ten Strike* had a small metal manikin that rolled a tiny ball down a bowling lane. The game was simple to play and understand, and took up much less space than conventional bowling machines and shuffle alleys because it was about the size of a pinball game.

Williams' *Ringer* was an arcade machine based on the game of horseshoes. You simply spun the control wheel on the front of the cabinet; as it turned, lights behind the glass would flash to indicate how close your pitch came to the stake. *Ringer* was created by veteran game designer Norm Clark despite the objections of the firm's marketing department, which thought the machine would be a disaster. After the prototype was completed, however, *Ringer* went into production and became one of the company's most popular novelty arcade machines.

On the other hand, Williams Electronics had high expectations for *Hyperball* (1982). Promoted as 'the next evolution of games', *Hyperball* lets you fire small steel balls at an array of targets inside a pinball-style cabinet. The machine's artwork was stunning, and *Hyperball* had good sound as well, but players just didn't like the concept. A similar machine called *Spellbinder* – designed as a follow-up to *Hyperball* – was killed in the prototype stage.

Another unusual Williams game was *Rat Race* (1984), a table-top maze game. *Rat Race* resembled a small wooden labyrinth toy, with a tilting playboard and several drop-through holes; the object was to roll a ball from one end of the maze to the other by

Grand Products introduced a new style of game it called 'Velocity Ball' when the company unveiled *Thunder Drome, Four Kings* and *Grand Baseball* in 1986. These machines had circular playfields, and invited you to release a rolling ball and send it spinning toward the targets. These Velocity Ball games played somewhat like pinball machines, but without the flippers. Players never quite felt comfortable with them, though.

tilting the playboard, being careful not to let the ball fall into the holes. *Rat Race* required a great deal of steady concentration and patience, but it was still deemed too passive by players accustomed to fast-moving video games.

Williams' *Crane* (1955) was different from other iron-claw diggers because it was designed for amusement only. Unlike most claw machines, Williams' *Crane* was filled with gravel rather than prizes. You operated four buttons that controlled a miniature steam shovel, and tried to scoop up as much gravel as possible before the clock ran out. The machine measured the amount of gravel that you moved, and rated your skill at the end of the game. Chicago Coin produced a gravel-digging machine of its own called *Steam Shovel* in the mid 1950s.

Americoin's *Junkyard* was similar to Williams' *Crane*, except that instead of gravel, you scooped up toy cars. Produced in the 1970s, *Junkyard* featured the 'fun sounds of crushing junk cars' as they dropped into the hopper, according to the company. *Junkyard* was larger than Williams' *Crane*, and even had two hoppers instead of just one.

Americoin's *Dozer* was an updated version of Williams' *Sidewalk Engineer*, but *Dozer* measured the amount of gravel that you moved, and awarded bonus playing time for high scores. *Dozer* had a bright green cabinet decorated with black stripes, and two large control handles to operate the bulldozer.

Americoin's *Fire Chief* let you squirt coloured water at several 'burning' targets. Simulated fires appeared in eight different windows of a four-storey home, and you operated a self-contained fire hose to extinguish the flames. A windshield wiper even cleaned the inside of the viewing glass! Americoin found that designing a game that used water was a mistake; leaks, evaporation and other problems were common on the machines.

Flys was another unusual Americoin game which let you use a real plastic fly swatter to wipe out these pests. 'A dirty fly buzzes around the playfield in rapid moving random patterns,' according to Americoin. 'When the fly lands and the buzzing stops, womp

ABOVE *Americoin built several novelty arcade games in the mid 1970s, including* Junkyard, *which was filled with die-cast metal 'junk' cars. The idea of this oddball game was to drop the wrecks into the hoppers of an auto-wrecking yard.*

him with your special fly swatter to get a score. You've got to be quick because flies are.'

Chicago Coin's *Hi-Score Pool* (1971) looked vaguely like a pinball machine, but it certainly didn't play

like one. The game had no bumpers, spinners or kickout holes; in fact, it had only a pair of flippers and 15 hollow, lighted pool balls suspended over the playfield. These pool balls lit up when the pinball rolled under them, and the object of the game was to keep the pinball in play long enough to light the entire rack of billiard balls. *Hi-Score Pool* forced you to break one of the most important rules of pinball – always keep your eye on the ball – because the pinball was concealed when it was near the top of the playfield under the pool balls. An interesting one-off, but the lack of scoring variation was a drawback.

Chicago Coin's *Criss Cross Pop Up* (1965), another game in a pinball style cabinet, let you play noughts and crosses (tic-tac-toe) with bouncing balls. A nine-square grid containing four rubber balls was reflected vertically in *Pop Up*'s backglass. Pushing the button on the front of the cabinet shot a pinball on to the playfield towards targets that launched some or all of the rubber balls. When the balls landed in the grid, you received points for various scoring combinations such as vertical rows and four corners, but quite often, the balls would land in scoreless arrangements. You received ten shots per game.

Exhibit Supply, founded in 1901, produced dozens of novelty arcade machines before the company went

out of business in the late fifties. Its range of peep show barrels was found in nearly every game room and amusement park in the 1940s and 1950s. Many of these machines had provocative titles guaranteed to pique your interest, but revealed an innocent visual gag rather than a racy or titillating scene. For example, who could resist a peep show barrel entitled 'A Collection of Shapely Pin-Ups'? It was only after you deposited your money that the inside of the barrel lit up to show a row of coloured clothes-pegs when you looked through the peephole.

But Exhibit's most unusual machine – in fact, one of the most bizarre coin-op machines ever produced by any manufacturer – was its 1957 *Nudist Colony*. The outside of this peep show viewer pictured the silhouette of a nude woman, and the words 'Nature

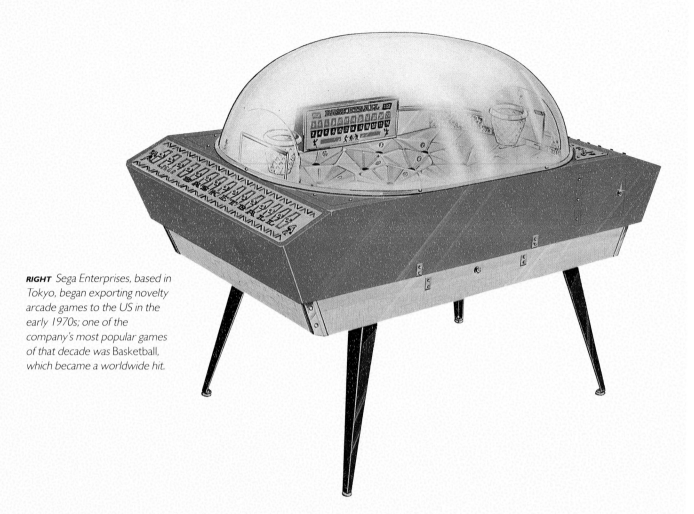

RIGHT *Sega Enterprises, based in Tokyo, began exporting novelty arcade games to the US in the early 1970s; one of the company's most popular games of that decade was* Basketball, *which became a worldwide hit.*

in the Raw, at Play and at Work'. But when you dropped in your nickel, you saw – ants! 'Exhibit's *Nudist Colony* is the greatest single attraction of the past ten years,' according to the company. 'People are drawn like a magnet. An entire colony of live ants living in a glass house. The colony is a complete ant city. In it are the streets, canals, storehouses, cemeteries and nurseries of the ants. Fascinating and profitable. With a minimum of care, the ants will live for years.' *Nudist Colony* sold for only $149 – rather inexpensive for an arcade machine, even in 1957 – but this clever coin-op idea wasn't enough to reverse Exhibit's sagging fortunes, and *Nudist Colony* was one of Exhibit's last machines.

J. F. Frantz Manufacturing has been building mechanical pellet shooting games since the 1920s; some of the company's machines, such as *US Marshall* and *Kicker and Catcher*, have been in production for decades without any major design

changes. You'll often find these non-electric machines in child-centred locations, although their nostalgic, old-fashioned design appeals to adults as well. Included among the company's recent games are *Coke Gallery* and *Pepsi Arcade*, which feature targets decorated with the popular soft drinks' logos.

Sega Enterprises of Tokyo, established in the 1960s, was the largest manufacturer of coin-op amusements outside the US. Although Sega's games were found in arcades throughout Europe and Asia, they weren't shipped to the US until the early 1970s. One of Sega's most popular machines was *Grand National*, which had a 3-D panoramic view of an old English countryside in a pinball-style cabinet. The scenery moved on a continuously rolling belt, and you controlled a horse which had to jump the approaching hurdles.

Sega's *Cowboy* was a rather unusual amusement game. You controlled an animated cowboy that was chasing a runaway steer across the open prairie, illuminated by black light. You controlled the cowboy's lasso, and tried to rope the steer by pressing the control button to release the rope at just the right moment.

Sega's *Motopolo* was a combination driving/table soccer game, and was one of the first machines the company sold in the US. *Motopolo* was played like polo, but instead of a horse, you manoeuvred a tiny remote-controlled motor bike around the playing field and tried to roll the ball into your opponent's goal.

Brunswick's *Karate* was unique because it required forceful, physical contact from players. You faced a large, plastic plate that pictured a lifesize reproduction of a martial arts expert; as selected areas of your opponent's body lit up, you had to strike – hard and fast – to get points. *Karate* was popular with young players – too popular, in fact, because the high-impact plastic plates had a tendency to shatter under the pounding.

In 1962, Midway Manufacturing released a pitch and bat game called *Target Gallery*. Instead of using a baseball theme like most pitch and bat machines, it pictured rabbits and squirrels on the backglass and playfield. With its 'cute' artwork, *Target Gallery* proved to be very popular, and Midway produced several similar games in the early sixties, including *2 Player Target Gallery* (with a 'cat and mouse' motif), *Carnival* (a circus-themed game) and *Mystery Score* (which pictured Frankenstein and other monsters gathered in a graveyard). Midway's *Winner* target gallery even featured two animated racing cars in the backbox. Hitting the targets advanced the cars up to four lengths, with scoring recorded in laps around the track. Only 1,500 machines were built, but the game remained popular for years.

THE ART OF THE GAME

You won't find any of the original backglass paintings from pinball machines hanging in the Louvre in Paris – not yet – but after decades of being taken for granted, the artwork on coin-op games is finally becoming a respected part of the machine.

As players' tastes have changed, the artwork on arcade amusements has evolved. In the 1930s and 1940s, many of the games had an art deco appearance, but by the 1950s, the illustrations took on a comic-book style. The artwork on many games of the 1960s was very angular, while the 1970s saw more detail and realism added to the art. Some manufacturers experimented with photographic backglasses on pinball machines in the eighties, but players preferred hand-drawn art.

Even the subjects pictured in the artwork have gradually changed. Before the 1970s, most players were male, and many games pictured large-breasted, scantily clad women to appeal to these players. But by the 1980s, coin-op games began using more 'wholesome' art as women played alongside men.

Each artist brings his own particular style or speciality to a game. Roy Parker illustrated many Gottlieb pinball games in the 1950s and 1960s including *Niagara*, *Happy Days* and *Egg Head*, and used a comic book style spiced with wit and hidden *double entendres*. Paul Faris drew some of Bally's most popular backglasses of the late 1970s, including *Lost World* and *Paragon*; many of his games have fantasy or superhero themes. And Kevin O'Connor, who created the artwork on several of Bally's 'celebrity' games like *Star Trek* and *Kiss*, is a master at portrait art.

There's an old proverb among game manufacturers which says that it's the artwork on a machine that gets the first coin from a player, but it's the game design that keeps him coming back. That philosophy still applies today, as the illustrations on coin-op amusement games are finally being recognized as contemporary works of art, and not simply something that fills the space on the glass.

RIGHT Zoltan, produced in the 1960s, featured a bearded old wizard that read your horoscope through a telephone receiver. Unlike the more elaborate gypsy fortune-telling machines of the past, Zoltan didn't move or breathe (although his crystal ball flashed when you inserted a coin).

Many old-time arcade novelties resurfaced in the 1950s, 1960s and 1970s. Gypsy fortune tellers remained popular arcade attractions, although they were less ornate than earlier models; the figures inside the machines often moved very mechanically, if they moved at all. Some of these new models were little more than vending machines that dispensed fortune cards or astrological forecasts.

One of the most innovative post-war fortune telling machines was *Morgana*, made by Bacchus Games. *Morgana* used black lighting and a concealed film projector to bring a mystical fortune teller to life. When you dropped in a quarter, a woman's face was projected inside the cabinet. As *Morgana* 'looked' at you, she told you about your future.

Old-fashioned strength and grip testers are still being produced today, and Zamperla, an Italian company, is the leading manufacturer of these machines. Zamperla's coin-op punching bags are popular around the world, while the company's *Bull* measures your strength as you squeeze the horns of a 3-D bull's head. Zamperla's most popular machine is *Mr. Muscle*, an arm wrestling game that features a life-sized 3-D moulded 'bully' with an outstretched arm that's hinged at the elbow. You can pick the level of resistance at the beginning of the game, so anyone can challenge *Mr. Muscle*.

One of today's most popular coin-op novelty games is *Whac-a-Mole*, produced by Bob's Space Racers. The game first appeared in the early seventies, and was an instant hit in arcades and amusement parks. Using a large padded 'hammer', you hit animated moles as they emerged from the five holes in the cabinet, with the moles moving faster as the game progressed. There's no strategy involved in playing *Whac-a-Mole*; you simply need a lot of concentration and quick reflexes. Namco of Japan produced a similar game called *Sweet Licks* which featured cute 'cake monsters' instead of burrowing moles.

'Hammering' machines would make for an interesting area of thematic collecting. Unfortunately, for obvious reasons, many such novelty games from the thirties and forties have not survived.

ABOVE *Midway's* Golden Arm *(1970) rated your strength from 'Weakling' to 'Piano Mover' to 'World's Champ'; the machine was particularly popular in blue-collar taverns.*

RIGHT Coin-operated recording booths – like this one by the International Mutoscope Corporation – were found in nearly every dime store, arcade and amusement park in the forties and fifties, although they are practically impossible to find nowadays.

Coin-operated photo booths were always one of the top arcade attractions, especially in the 1950s, before Polaroid photography became common. For a half a dollar, you could have four different poses taken and developed in less than three minutes. Some people used the photos for identification, but they were especially popular with young couples out on a date. Small children also found that unoccupied photo booths, with their dark curtains that covered the doorways, made great playrooms.

As instant cameras became more common, photo booths began offering gag pictures. Atari's 1975 *Compugraph Foto* machine printed life-sized portraits on computer paper, while *Photovideo* by I.O. Inc. gave your pictures 'fun house' mirror effects. *The*

Amazing Photo Booth by Amazing Photos 'lets the customer fulfill their photo fantasies by choosing their own background for the photograph,' according to the maker. Several companies, including Polaroid, still produce 'traditional' photo booths, though.

Coin-op recording booths were very popular in the 1940s and 1950s, but they're nearly impossible to find today. You could record a short message – usually about two minutes long – on a six-inch cardboard record for about 35 cents. You even heard your recording played back before you left the booth. The last recording booths were produced by the International Mutoscope Company in 1968. When portable tape recorders became popular in the 1970s, coin-op recording booths started to vanish.

LEFT For years, people have been writing their own personalized messages on round metal discs on Identification Medal machines like this one. These souvenir tokens have raised lettering and are often attached to key rings.

BELOW *It isn't hard to guess what served as the inspiration for All-Tech's 1966* Bat Car *kiddie ride.*

RIGHT *It may look like Donald, but this kiddie ride from the early 1950s is called* Dopey Duck. *Most children probably couldn't tell the difference between Dopey and the popular Disney character, though.*

Penny presses were another popular arcade novelty. These machines stamped 'The Lord's Prayer' or other sayings on an ordinary penny while you waited. The pressed pennies were elongated and worthless when they came out of the machines, but they made interesting souvenirs. Actually, many of these penny presses didn't really return the same penny that you inserted, but instead gave you a 'pre-pressed' coin.

Token or medal stampers have also been around for years. These machines let you print a few words on a round, metal disc, which you could keep for a lasting souvenir.

Arcades have always held a special magic for children, and some companies specialize in coin-op amusements designed just for youngsters. Kiddie rides have been popular for years because they offer children the same thrills that adults get at amusement parks. Some kiddie rides resembled helicopters and rocket ships and rose two or three feet into the air, while mechanical pony rides that simulated the feeling of riding a bucking bronco were also popular. Practically every sort of animal and vehicle was featured on at least one kiddie ride. Children could pick from *Porpy the Porpoise, Rudy the Deer* or *Porky the Pig.* Or they might prefer riding in the *Ben Hur Chariot, Hot-Rod Racer* or *Sea Skate Speedboat.*

Kiddie rides often reflected national trends. Cowboy wagons and pony rides were hot in the early fifties when westerns were popular on television, but by the end of the decade, children preferred rocket and spaceship rides.

In the 1960s, some kiddie rides included amusement games. All-Tech's *Indian Scout* horse ride, for instance, featured an electronic pistol and target box specially designed for children, while *Cross Country Racer* was actually a scaled-down driving game.

stories ranging from fairy tales to westerns to 'Bozo the Clown' stories. 'Youngest toddler and busiest parent get the *Fun-Phone* idea at a glance,' according to Bally's promotional literature. 'When coin is deposited, youngster picks up receiver, and hears a pleasant voice tell one of a dozen clever stories recorded on a built-in tape player.'

Chicago Coin's *Round the World Trainer* (1956) was described by the company as a 'gun ride for adults'. You sat in a control car and turned a steering wheel to aim a light gun attached to the front of the car, at an electronic map of the world mounted a few feet away. There were 20 numbered cities, states and countries on the map, and you had to shoot a light beam at each of them – one by one, in the numbered order – in less than a minute. The control car moved as you turned the steering wheel to give you the sensation of flying 'round the world'. The game was even weatherproof for outdoor locations.

Another game pitched at adults was *The Stripper*, produced in the seventies by Universal Products. A photo of a fully clothed model appeared on the screen at the start of the game, along with a continuously moving bullseye target. Hitting the bullseye removed a piece of clothing, and 15 hits revealed everything. *The Stripper*'s projector held 80 slides and featured five different models, so you could play the machine several times before seeing the same model twice. *The Stripper* operated on a clock, rather than giving you a predetermined number of shots. The game never really had a chance to attract players, though, since many amusement operators found that *The Stripper* violated their local anti-pornography laws.

Game manufacturers never know how a machine will fare before it's released. No matter how original or innovative a game is, it's often impossible to predict whether the machine will become a hit or a flop. Edcoe's *Computer Tic Tac Toe*, produced in the mid 1970s, probably sounded great on paper – a two-player table-top game with an electronic noughts and crosses (tic-tac-toe) board in the centre. Most players, however, preferred to play the game for free, on paper, as Edcoe learned the hard way.

ABOVE Children loved Bimbo, *the dancing marionette produced by United Billiards in the 1970s. This coin-op toy was based on Williams' popular* Peppy the Clown *(1956).*

Another coin-op amusement designed just for children was Williams' *Peppy the Clown*, an animated marionette produced in 1955. Children could move Peppy's arms and legs and make him dance along to the calliope music played by the machine. *Peppy the Clown* was one of the most popular arcade novelties produced specifically for youngsters, although several other companies have also built coin-op marionettes and puppet theatres.

Bally's *Fun-Phone* (1960) was designed for children aged three to 12, and was billed by the company as a 'junior jukebox'. This bright red device looked like a pay telephone, but played pre-recorded children's

LEFT *When television was in its infancy in the late 1940s, I.J. Manufacturing's TV Viewer offered you the chance to see what you would look like on the screen. The company also produced* The Echo Phone, *which let you hear your own voice over a telephone.*

On the other hand, coin-op basketball machines are one of the hottest novelty games around. These 10ft×10ft×3ft games use 7-inch basketballs, and give you about a minute to shoot as many baskets as you can. The popularity of these machines surprised many experts in the coin-op games industry, who initially viewed them as having very limited appeal.

Some coin-op games that were developed in the fifties, sixties and seventies – such as air hockey – have become perennial arcade favourites and not just short-lived novelties, while others that were expected to remain popular for years have disappeared without a trace. As future generations of players come to discover the magic of arcades, we're sure to see new coin-op novelties that will amuse and amaze us.

WHEN THE PLUG WAS PULLED...

Some coin-op games never made it into the arcades. For a variety of reasons, the games listed here never got past the prototype stage. In most cases, only two or three samples of each of these machines were built – and most of these prototypes were destroyed when the games were abandoned.

★ Bally's *Hot Shotz* (1987) An ill-fated combination of pinball and pool. Instead of a small silver ball, you flipped a full-sized cue ball around the green felt-covered playfield and tried to hit several 'captive' billiard balls.

★ Williams' *Kickapoo II* (1984) An update of the company's 1965 *Kickapoo* shuffle targette game, *Kickapoo II* was a cross between a puck bowler and a skee ball machine. Instead of bowling pins, *Kickapoo II* had several scoring cups at the end of the lane.

★ Game Plan's *Loch Ness Monster* (1985) Possibly the best pinball machine created by this now defunct manufacturer. *Loch Ness Monster* was one of the first games to include a jackpot feature, along with a miniature sea serpent under the playfield. Shortly after producing the prototype, Game Plan went bankrupt.

★ Stern's *Pitchman* (1983) Only one prototype was built of this laser disc game, which featured film footage of a sharply dressed actor portraying a magician named Dr Slye. By the time the prototype was finished, the laser disc fad had come and gone, and the game was shelved.

★ Atari's *Monza* (1979) The only sit-down cocktail table pinball from this company. Shortly after Atari introduced *Monza*, the company left the pinball field to concentrate on its video games.

★ Williams' *Predators* (1984) Actually four video games in one. *Predators* was an outer space 'shoot and dodge' game that used four separate cabinets, connected by electronic cables. Up to four players could take part, with each seeing the action from their own perspective.

★ Stern's *Lazerlord* (1984) In an attempt to re-enter the pinball market after a three-year absence, Stern re-released its 1980 *Quicksilver* pin under a new name and with different artwork. Only one *Lazerlord* prototype was built.

★ Gottlieb/Premier's *Hoopz* (1985) The only novelty arcade game from this long-time pinball company. *Hoopz* was a basketball-themed machine, with two player-controlled metal manikins inside a glass-enclosed cabinet.

★ Bally's *Mysterian* (1984) This unusual pinball machine was designed for 'southpaws', with the plunger on the left side of the cabinet. Bally built only one *Mysterian* before killing the game.

★ Williams' *Still Crazy* (1984) A sort of vertical pinball game with six flippers. The object was to relay the marble-sized steel balls from the bottom of the field to the top, and flip them into the hillbilly's jug of moonshine whiskey.

RIGHT *Some games never make it into arcades; Premier Technology built only one prototype sample of this* Hoopz *basketball game which was housed in a glass dome.*

CHAPTER 9

Owning Your Own . . .

When you think about arcade games, you probably picture a large games room filled with rows of noisy machines and people lined up to play them. While it's true that coin-operated games are designed to provide years of entertainment in arcades, more and more of them are turning up in private homes.

Arcade games make great conversation pieces. They brighten up any recreation room, and a few are good investments, too, especially with the current demand for nostalgia and collectibles. There's a satisfying feeling in looking at a machine in your home, and thinking about all the pleasure that it has brought to hundreds of players before you.

There's something special about being able to play your own machine any time you want, without having to go to an arcade. Your game is always there

BELOW *The stunning ancient Egyptian artwork on Williams Electronics' 1981* King Tut *shuffle bowling machine will add a touch of class to any recreation room. Whatever your interests, you're likely to find a game that's perfect for you.*

RIGHT *If you're a fan of comic characters, you might want a 1984 Gottlieb* Three Stooges *video game in your collection — if you can find one. Coin-op*

games based on movies and TV shows are usually in great demand because they're often sought-after by motion picture buffs.

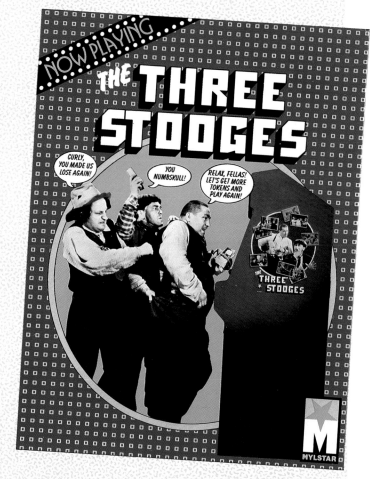

for you whenever you want to forget your problems and escape from the world around you.

No matter what your interests, there's an arcade game out there for you. Do you play chess? If you do, you might enjoy Midway's *Checkmate* video. Are you an old movie buff? Then Chicago Coin's *Cinema* pinball might be perfect for you. If you're fascinated with ancient Egyptian art, Williams' *King Tut* shuffle alley could be just the machine to suit your tastes.

If your recreation room has a specific motif, you can select something that blends in with the decor. For instance, if your room has a nautical theme, you might want a game like Bally's *Fathom* pinball or Williams' *Aqua Gun* rifle. Or if you recreation room is decorated with baseball memorabilia, Chicago Coin's *Batter Up* baseball or Midway's *Extra Inning* video game would be ideal.

Television and movie fans can pick from dozens of games ranging from Gottlieb's *Dragonette* pinball (a parody of the 'Dragnet' TV series) to Data East's *The Simpsons* pinball (featuring the stars of today's cartoon hit). Quite a few machines of the seventies and eighties were based on TV shows and movies, including Gottlieb's *Charlie's Angels* pinball, Sega's *Star Trek* video, Bally's *Six Million Dollar Man* pinball, Gottlieb's *Three Stooges* video and Atari's *Indiana Jones and the Temple of Doom* video. There's even a video game based on a TV game show (Sente's *Name That Tune!*) and another based on a board game (Sente's *Trivial Pursuits*).

Before you get a machine, though, you should carefully consider what type of game to buy. If your space is limited, for example, a 16-foot ball bowling machine will not be practical. Or if you have young children in your home, you'll probably want something that appeals to their tastes along with your own.

Whatever game you decide to buy, be sure to play it first – several times, if possible – because you want to be certain that the game will hold your int-

erest for a long time. Don't take someone else's word that a game is 'great fun' to play; a machine that appeals to one person might put another to sleep. Many mechanical arcade games lose their appeal after a few weeks because they become repetitive. Driving games, for instance, often use films to project the streets and background scenery, and if you play these games enough, you can literally play them blindfolded. And while coin-operated trivia and quiz games are entertaining, you certainly won't want to see the same questions cropping up again and again.

Many pre-war machines are magnificent to look at but have little long-term play appeal. For instance, it's fascinating to watch a gypsy fortune teller machine in operation; they are among the most sought-after coin-op devices, but the reason for this is almost purely aesthetic.

Ideally, your machine should have some element of randomness (or luck) built into it. This keeps the game interesting over the long run. Remember, arcade machines (especially those built before the 1970s) were designed so that players could master them and then move on to another game. Manufacturers assumed that players would tire of shooting at the same 'pop-up' target on a rifle game or circling the same grand prix racetrack on a driving game.

Some coin-op games offer multiple playing strategies; for example, most bowling machines include four or five different game choices besides regulation scoring to challenge you continually. Other mechanical arcade machines get progressively more difficult the better you become, which helps keep the game interesting. Bally's *Ball Park* baseball machine, for instance, pitches the ball faster and more unpredictably as your score increases. Just be sure all of the features on your game are working properly. A bowling machine that has a pin that doesn't register is always galling.

It's always fun to compete against someone else on an arcade game, and you can find many head-to-head machines out there. Chicago Coin's *Twin Rifle*, for example, lets two players shoot at the same moving targets, with points awarded to the marksman who hits it first. Like the majority of multi-player games, *Twin Rifle* can also be played by one person against the clock.

Shuffle alleys are ideal for home use because most people already know the basic rules of bowling, and the games can accommodate up to six people. Shuffle alleys play fast – the average game lasts only about a minute – so even if you have a crowd in your recreation room, everyone can have a turn at taking on the machine.

Gun games are also fun for everyone, and most of them don't take up much space. While small children may have some difficulty mastering the hand–eye coordination needed to play, nearly everyone will want to test their marksmanship.

Mechanical pinball machines come in one-, two- and four-player models, while nearly every electronic game is designed for up to four players. Pinball is a game that everyone can enjoy, because even if you're not a hardcore pinball fanatic, it's easy to understand

the basic objective of keeping the ball on the playfield and hitting the targets. There's a combination of skill and luck incorporated into every machine's design, so even a novice can sometimes enjoy the thrill of beating a more experienced player.

Several arcade-style pinball machines were produced strictly for home use, and Bally was the leading manufacturer of these games. Some of these machines had the same names as their coin-op counterparts, but completely different playfield layouts. If you buy Bally's *Fireball*, *Captain Fantastic* or *Evel Knievel* pinballs, be sure that you're getting the coin-operated version and not the scaled-down home model.

ABOVE It's more fun to compete! Games that let two players compete head-to-head mean that your friends can join in and make owning your own machine more fun.

ABOVE *Bally produced home versions of some of its most popular commercial pinball machines including Captain Fantastic and Fireball, so be sure that you're getting a coin-operated machine if that's what you're paying for.*

Cocktail table games are ideal for home use. Many have rich, hardwood cabinets that make them look like fine furniture. These sit-down games can even be covered with a tablecloth and used like an ordinary cocktail table! On the other hand, large cockpit-style video games are often too bulky for domestic enjoyment. Teenagers (and young children) would probably enjoy having one around, though, because cockpit games surround you with sight and sound for an effect that you just can't normally get with home video games. Unfortunately, these machines do not come cheaply.

RIGHT *Many coin-op games were produced in a cocktail-table format, such as Allied Leisure's Take Five (1978), the first such pinball machine. These games take up less space than full-sized arcade machines, and blend into the decor of nearly any home games room.*

Some coin-operated games just aren't practical for home use. For example, air hockey tables are large and heavy, and require two people to play. Likewise, you need two players for foosball; moreover, non coin-op foosball tables are smaller and lighter than arcade models, and often play almost as well.

You might prefer buying an older electromechanical arcade game for your home. These were last produced in 1977, and most are now in private homes and collectors' hands. Prices for these older machines vary widely, depending on the game and its condition. The 'flying bomber' games from the sixties and seventies, such as Chicago Coin's *Sky Battle* and Allied Leisure's *Sonic Fighter*, have very little value; you can often buy them for about $50 (£25).

Early *Pong*-style video games are probably the least expensive coin-op machines to buy – and the least interesting to play. Most videos produced before about 1975 have very rudimentary ping pong-type action, far simpler than even the most basic home video game system. A few years ago, some game operators and distributors were giving these outdated videos free to customers with the purchase of newer machines, just to rid their warehouses of out-of-date stock; other distributors simply hauled them out to the rubbish tip.

On the other hand, some novelty arcade games (including Genco's *Two-Player Basketball*) often sell for more than $3,000 (£1,500). Parts (such as back-glasses) for these old games are today nearly impossible to find in good shape, though, and even potentially priceless machines are literally worthless if they're incomplete or in poor condition.

One of the best ways to find a mechanical arcade game is by reading the classified sales ads in your local newspaper, because many home-owners advertise old machines that have been sitting in a corner of their basement for years. Yard and garage sales may also yield occasional finds, although quite often, machines purchased from private homes may need minor repairs. Antique and second-hand thrift stores may also have coin-op games for sale, usually in 'as is' condition.

You might want to buy a favourite game that you remember playing when you were younger. Finding a specific machine may not be easy, though, because some games had very limited production runs, especially those made in the 1950s and early 1960s. Although no precise figures are available, some game collectors estimate that only about five to 10 per cent of a game's production run survives after 25 years; in fact, only two or three specimens of several rare pre-1970 coin-op games are known to exist today, so finding a specific machine from the fifties or sixties may be close to impossible.

There are several places where you can go to buy a machine for your home. If you're looking for a recent pinball or video game, you may find it at your local arcade. However, these machines are often the newest, top-earning games and priced out of the range of most private game enthusiasts. In the US recent machines can be found at game distributors, located in just about every major city. These distributors are usually listed in the Yellow Pages under 'Amusement Devices' and most have an assortment of new and used machines available, cleaned up and working perfectly. Most distributors can even arrange for delivery.

You can expect to pay at least $300 (£150) if you buy a reconditioned machine from a distributor – with new games priced at $2,500 (£1,250) and more. Most distributors even guarantee reconditioned games for up to 90 days. This 'insurance' can be valuable, especially if you don't know much yourself about the ins and outs of game repair.

Newer electronic arcade games – whether they're pinball machines, video games or shuffle alleys – usually have fewer service problems than older mechanical games. Most distributors (and some operators) have technicians that make home service calls, although most of these mechanics work only with electronic machines and may not be trained to work on older games.

Auctions can be an excellent source for good used games. The machines are often reconditioned and tested, and you'll probably even have a chance to

LEFT Games that feature mechanical animation – like Chicago Coin's 1961 Pro Basketball – are highly sought-after by collectors, and are rapidly going up in value.

monthly publication that offers repair tips and information about jukeboxes and Coke machines as well as amusement games.

Don't buy an arcade game strictly as an investment, with the intention of selling it for a profit someday. Coin-operated games are similar to vintage cars; a few may become classics (like the '57 Chevy) but most do not appreciate in value significantly. While some collectors will pay high prices for specific machines, you should buy a game strictly because you enjoy playing it.

Because coin-op games are made for commercial use, they're not readily portable. The average weight of one of these games is about 250 to 300 lbs (110 to 135 kg), and most machines can be moved by two people with the aid of a handcart. You'll probably need a van, pick-up truck or small trailer if you plan to transport the game yourself. Remember, too, to check the dimensions of any doors and stairways in your home, to make sure it can get through.

By the way, while a few arcade machines can be set on free play, most require a coin to start the game. Don't worry, though, about how many games you play, because you'll be able to reach inside your machine and retrieve your money any time you want to, a luxury that you'll never have in any arcade!

If you can't afford your own coin-op game (or just don't have the space), you might want to display arcade-related memorabilia in your home. Some amusement game enthusiasts decorate their walls with backglasses from their favourite machines. These colourful souvenirs are a genuine piece of nostalgia that anyone can afford. You can even purchase original colour sales brochures (suitable for framing) for most arcade games.

No matter what game you ultimately bring home, it will be special because it will be yours. A word of caution, though – arcade games multiply when you bring them home. Start with one, and before long, they'll be taking over the house!

play them before the bidding starts. Most of these auctions offer electronic pinball and video games that are from two to ten years old, with most games selling for between $100 (£50) and $1,200 (£600).

Some American cities also have retail stores that sell 'rec room' equipment, including pool tables and darts games, along with used coin-op arcade machines. They offer professionally reconditioned games, but you'll probably have to shell out a lot of money for them. Nevertheless, you'll have the assurance of knowing that you're buying an expertly restored game.

If you're looking for a specific machine, you should try one of the collectors' journals. The *Pinball Trader* is a monthly newsletter that includes articles and features about pinballs, bowlers, baseballs and other coin-op games, along with several pages of classified ads from collectors. *Gameroom* magazine is another

SPECIAL COLLECTIBLES

Having an arcade game in your home can give you hours of enjoyment, but you might be surprised to find out that your machine's value has changed since you bought it.

The market for used coin-op games is very fluid. What's hot now may be junk in the future, while today's cast offs may be tomorrow's treasures. In the late 1950s, for example, when 45 rpm records were becoming popular, nobody wanted the obsolete jukeboxes from the forties that played 78s, and many game distributors sold them for as little as $15, just to clean out their warehouses. Today, these old jukeboxes – such as the 'classic' Wurlitzer 1015 with its coloured lights and bubble tubes – cost $10,000 to $12,000 (£5,000 to £6,000).

Games that feature popular entertainers or are based on TV shows and movies often increase in value. Williams' 1967 *Beat Time* pinball pictures 'The Bootles' on the backglass, making it a highly prized collectible among Beatles fans. Bally's *Wizard* and *Captain Fantastic* pinballs – both based on the 1975 film *Tommy* – also command top prices.

Some collectors look for 'first' games – the first electronic shuffle bowling game (Williams' 1978 *Topaz*), the first pinball machine with flippers (Gottlieb's 1947 *Humpty Dumpty*) or the first game ever produced by a large manufacturer, such as Atari's 1972 *Pong* video game.

The demand for some games often exceeds the supply. Bally's *Pac Man* video had a record-setting production run, but when players got tired of it after a few years, operators converted many of them into different higher-earning games by simply replacing the old computer chips with new ones and repainting the cabinets. There just aren't enough original *Pac Man* machines left intact to satisfy the demand for this classic game, so the price is slowly rising.

Some collectors look for rare, low-production games, while others prefer the nostalgic appeal and artwork of machines built in the 1950s. Nearly every game fits into someone's collection somewhere. Because everyone has different tastes in coin-op games, every machine is potentially collectible.

RIGHT *Some collectors look for unique games like* Paddle Ball *(1973), the first video game produced by Williams. The company went on to produce a string of video hits in the 1980s.*

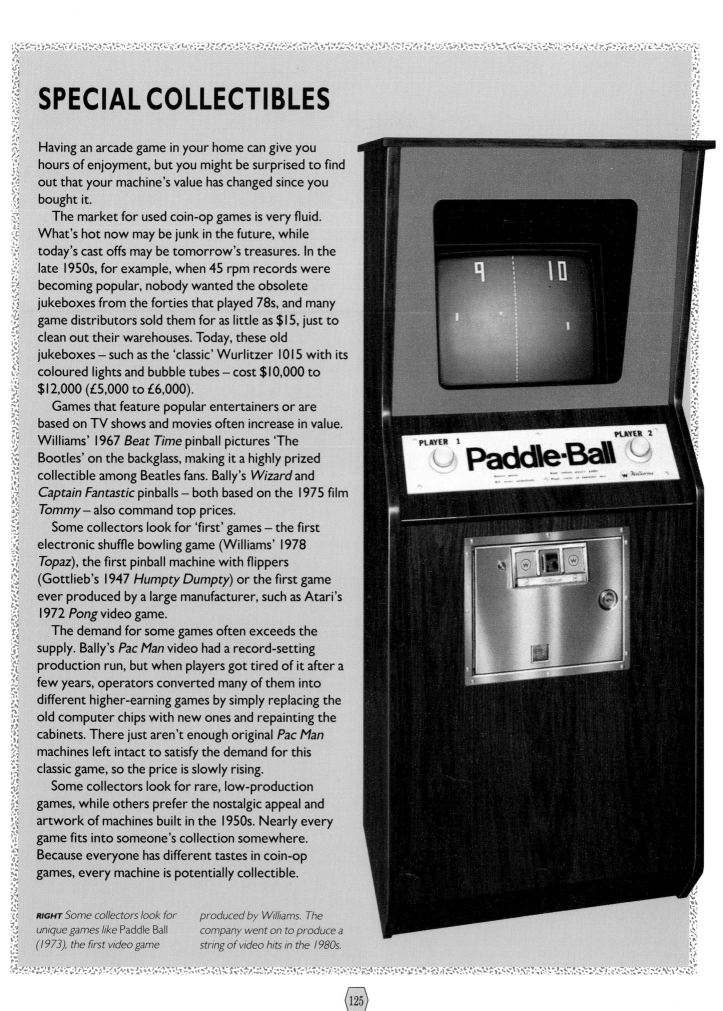

INDEX

ACKNOWLEDGEMENTS

The author would like to acknowledge the following people for their contributions to this book:

MICHAEL CARBONE, Carousel Arcade, Seaside Heights, New Jersey; DAN CLARTON, Premier Technology, Bensenville, Illinois; NICK COCHIS, Boston, Massachusetts; FEDERICO CROCI, Bologna, Italy; DENNIS DODEL, The Pinball Trader, Brentwood, Missouri; BALINT KOCSIS, Honolulu, Hawaii; STEVE KORDEK, Williams Electronics Games, Chicago, Illinois; BERNARD MARROU, Avignon, France; WILLIAM 'BANG' MEYER, Oxford, Ohio; GARY PHILLIPS, Seaside Heights, New Jersey; JEFF SIEGEL, Cincinnati, Ohio; HERB SILVERS, Fabulous Fantasies, Los Angeles, California; HORST SOLLNER, Immenreuth, Germany; MARVIN YAGODA, Marvin's Marvelous Mechanical Museum, Farmington Hills, Michigan. *And very special thanks to my wife Fran for all of her help and patience*